American and English Fiction in the Nineteenth Century

Nicolaus Mills

American and English Fiction in the Nineteenth Century

AN ANTIGENRE CRITIQUE AND COMPARISON

INDIANA UNIVERSITY PRESS
Bloomington / London

For

Marvin Felheim
John Seidman
Hyatt Waggoner

Contents

Acknowledgments

The debts I have tried to acknowledge with my dedication are only the beginning. I want to thank Alice Bloom, David Hirsch, Ross Miller, and John Wright for their readings, and my editors at Indiana University Press, John Gallman and Margaret Rhea, for their willingness to fight with me. The University of Michigan supplied me with a Rackham Grant during a summer when I really needed the free time and the dough.

I would also like to acknowledge permission from three journals to reprint material from previously published articles. Chapter one appeared in a somewhat different version as "American Fiction and the Genre Critics" in the Winter 1969 issue of *Novel: A Forum on Fiction.* Chapter four is a revision of "The Discovery of Nil in *Pierre* and *Jude the Obscure,*" which appeared in the Summer 1970 issue of *Texas Studies in Literature and Language,* published by the University of Texas Press. Cambridge University Press kindly allowed me to use parts of "Social and Moral Vision in *Great Expectations* and *Huckleberry Finn,*" from the July 1970 issue of the *Journal of American Studies.*

American and English Fiction in the Nineteenth Century

Introduction

In the preface to his study of *The Romance in America*, Joel Porte writes:

> Thanks to a series of major critical studies that have appeared in the past decade and a half, it no longer seems necessary to argue for the importance of romance as a nineteenth-century American genre. Students of American literature—notably Richard Chase—have provided a solid theoretical basis for establishing that the rise and growth of fiction in this country is dominated by our authors' conscious adherence to a tradition of non-realistic romance sharply at variance with the broadly novelistic mainstream of English writing. When there has been disagreement among recent critics as to the contours of American fiction, it has usually disputed, not the existence per se of a romantic tradition, but rather the question of which authors, themes, and stylistic strategies deserve to be placed with certainty at the heart of that tradition.[1]

Porte's description of the path modern studies of American fiction have as a rule followed is, I believe, accurate.[2] It is the path itself that I find misleading, and my first aim in this study is to show that we cannot classify American fiction as romantic and English fiction as novelistic and on that basis accurately distinguish between the two traditions. American fiction is not so free from societal concerns and English fiction is not so weighted down with history that such a comparison makes sense. Nor is it possible, I think, to get around this difficulty by arguing that "most of the great American novels are romances, most of the English novels are not."[3] The problem of distinguishing American fiction from English fiction also cannot be resolved by using statistical yardsticks, which may or may not be relevant to a particular novel and indicate nothing whatsoever about textual balance or variations within a tradition.

As it applies to a series of critical studies on the nature and the uniqueness of American fiction, my argument is, to be sure, deflationary. I find the similarities far more important and the differences far less important between nineteenth-century American and English fiction than is customary. But my argument is not deflationary with respect to the novels in question. For what I am contending is that these works have a complexity that defies easy categorization and makes it necessary to see their uniqueness in far subtler ways than their division into genres allows. Such an interpretation does not require wholesale abandonment of the many specific insights into American fiction that the criticism of the last twenty-five years has provided. But it does call for a revaluation of American fiction in terms of a broad, comparative framework.[4] And it does stand in direct opposition to the kind of analysis that allows a contemporary scholar like Christopher Ricks to quote with approval William Hazlitt's observation of 150 years ago: "The map of America is not historical; and therefore works of fiction do not take root in it; for the fiction, to be good for anything, must not be in the author's mind, but belong to the age or country in which he lives. The genius of America is essentially mechanical and modern."[5]

In contrast to Professor Porte my starting point is not with Richard Chase's *The American Novel and its Tradition* but with Lionel Trilling's *The Liberal Imagination.* I believe that David Hirsch is correct when he writes of Trilling's seminal influence, "Two generations of students of American literature must acknowledge a deep debt to Lionel Trilling. . . . Such books as Richard Chase's *The American Novel and its Tradition,* Marius Bewley's *The Eccentric Design,* and Leslie Fiedler's *Love and Death in the American Novel* would hardly have been possible had not Mr. Trilling pointed the way."[6] Especially in his essays, "Manners, Morals, and the Novel" and "Art and Fortune," Professor Trilling has laid the groundwork for seeing

American fiction as romantic, its concerns as overwhelmingly ideal-
istic, and its major preoccupations as "tangential to society."[7]

Trilling's weaknesses, particularly his emphasis on manners, have
been explored in painstaking fashion by Delmore Schwartz in his
essay, "The Duchess' Red Shoes," from which I quote:

> Mr. Trilling began his essay by saying that what he meant by manners
> was virtually indefinable. He continued by making a series of assertions
> which were intended to substitute a kind of circumscription for a defini-
> tion: he did not mean "the rules of personal intercourse in our culture;
> and yet such rules were by no means irrelevant" nor did he mean "man-
> ners in the sense of *mores*, customs," although that meaning was also
> relevant. "What I understand by manners, then, is a culture's hum and
> buzz of implication . . . that part of culture which is made up of half-
> uttered or unuttered or unutterable expressions of value . . . the things
> that for good or bad draw the people of a culture together." This is Mr.
> Trilling's broad definition of manners, namely the manners of particular
> social classes and groups in a given social hierarchy. It is by moving back
> and forth between his broad (and tentative) definition and his limited
> (and unexpressed) definition that Mr. Trilling is able to hold forth *Don
> Quixote* as a true novel (here the broad definition works) while *The Scarlet
> Letter* (here it is the limited definition) suffers "from a lack of social
> texture" and is, like almost all American novels, not concerned with
> society at all. How can one say, in terms of Mr. Trilling's broad definition,
> that *The Scarlet Letter, Moby Dick*, and *Huckleberry Finn* lack social texture?
> The equivalent would be to say that *Walden* is not about society because
> it deals with a solitary individual. In the same way, again, it is only by
> using his limited definition and ignoring his broad one that Mr. Trilling
> can quote and agree with James Fenimore Cooper and Henry James on
> "the thick social texture of English life and the English novel" in the
> nineteenth centruy as opposed to the thinness of American life and the
> American novel: for in terms of his broad definition there was just as
> much social texture in America as in England; it was a different social
> texture as it was a different society and it was not the kind of social
> texture that James was interested in: but it had just as much of "a cul-
> ture's hum and buzz of implication," etc., which Mr. Trilling says he
> means by manners.[8]

To continue, however, with Mr. Trilling's positive recommendations:
"Now the novel as I have described it has never really established itself
in America. Not that we have not had great novels, but that the novel in
America diverges from its classic intention which, as I have said, is the

investigation of reality beginning in the social field. The fact is that American writers of genius have not turned their minds to society." This latter sentence makes sense only if Mr. Trilling gives a very limited meaning to the word, society. This becomes clear when Mr. Trilling explains why American writers have turned away from "society": "Americans have a kind of reluctance to looking closely at society. They appear to believe that to touch upon a matter of class is somehow to demean ourselves." Which is to say that unless one is concerned with class and snobbery one is not really concerned with "society."[9]

My criticism of *The Liberal Imagination* is not nearly so detailed as Delmore Schwartz's, however, for although I believe Lionel Trilling is responsible for initiating a series of critical misreadings of American fiction, the problems that concern me go beyond the range of his essays.

In order to examine these problems systematically I have divided this study into a series of essays that offer both a practical and a theoretical definition of the uniqueness of nineteenth-century American fiction. In Chapter One I begin by reviewing the literary and historical grounds on which I believe previous approaches to the subject have gone wrong and then argue for a reading of American fiction that is comparative and takes into account its full dimension. In the next four chapters I try to make explicit this general proposition through an analysis of eight English and American novels. With Scott and Cooper I focus on the implications of their historical vision. In the case of Hawthorne and Eliot my concern is with their treatment of the religious dilemma of the fall. I compare Melville and Hardy in terms of their preoccupation with the concept of nil. With Dickens and Twain I emphasize the relationship they see between the brutalization of children and the dehumanization of society. Each of these essays is intended to stand independently, but I believe their overall effect is to reveal a common pattern of similarity and variation in the books discussed. In my conclusion I attempt to put this common pattern into perspective and to suggest where it leads. The appendices to this study are intended to supplement the critical discussion of Chapter One. They involve studies with which I am in much greater agreement. In the first appendix I examine Richard Bridgman's and Richard Poirier's essays on style in American fiction, and in the second I evaluate revisions in the Trilling thesis suggested by A.N. Kaul.

I have thought this study best served by examining closely a limited number of texts and generalizing from them rather than using a greater number of texts but offering necessarily less detailed analyses. I have, as a result, focused on writers who, it is generally assumed, reflect the major tradition in nineteenth-century American and English fiction and then selected for comparison a representative work of each.[10] But I would be less than candid if I did not acknowledge certain dissatisfactions with this method and express the hope that in the not-too-distant future we will see efforts toward a much broader comparative study of American and English fiction. The only book I have discussed that seems to me of questionable merit is Herman Melville's *Pierre*. I have made this choice partly because I think that *Moby Dick*, like *The Brothers Karamazov* or *Ulysses*, tends to dominate any comparative setting in which it appears and also because I believe that, as Charles Feidelson has noted, "Defective as it is, *Pierre*, not *Moby Dick*, is the best vantage point for a general view of Melville's work. In *Pierre* his fundamental artistic problem is more baldly stated and more fully conceived, even as it becomes more damaging to his artistic self-confidence."[11] Henry James has not been treated as an American because his fiction is so often conceded to reflect a mixture of novelistic and romantic qualities that to include him in my argument would be to go over uncontested territory.

I have deliberately compared nineteenth-century American and English fiction at the points where the two traditions are closest on the grounds that the distinctions that can be observed here are the only ones that apply generally. The eight novels on which this study is based are not paired in strict chronological order, however. I do not find a consistent line of development that explains American or English fiction, and I think it evident that, despite the years separating their work, writers like Melville and Hardy often have more in common than writers who were more nearly contemporaries. Similarly, there has been no deliberate effort to pair writers who were familiar with each other's work. When their comments are relevant, I have noted the remarks that writers I compare have made about each other, but the kinds of problems with which this study is concerned are illuminated only secondarily by such criticism.

I have limited the period covered in this book to the nineteenth century because I find that after D.H. Lawrence it is virtually impossible to draw significant, major distinctions between American and English fiction. Lawrence, as his *Studies of Classic American Literature* demonstrates, possessed an acute understanding of the tensions between visionary and societal concerns that shaped American fiction, and more importantly, he struggled with similar tensions in his own novels, which are structured like American fiction. This pattern is especially clear in a novella like *St. Mawr*, where Lawrence not only delves into the very questions on time and space that preoccupied American writers in the nineteenth century but shifts his setting from the confines of England to the desert of New Mexico. The same pattern is present in Lawrence's writing from the beginning, however, as one can see from *Sons and Lovers*, where Paul Morel achieves a Whitmanesque sense of himself as "less than an ear of wheat lost in the field. . . . at the core a nothingness, and yet not nothing."[12]

Finally, while I have no wish to apologize for the often polemical quality of this book, I must emphasize that I think asking the question, What is unique about American fiction? does not in the long run mean engaging in a narrow, academic quarrel, but trying to discover whether or not the visionary concerns so vital to American fiction are what Tony Tanner has called "unearned generalizations."[13] The relationship between these problems of uniqueness and fullness seems to me of paramount importance, and in the essays that follow I hope to provide a bridge between them. The corrective that I offer to what in the last twenty-five years has become the standard school of thought on American fiction is not intended to close out debate on the subject but to make it less one-sided, to provide a more concrete, less restrictive view of the worth of American fiction.

NOTES

1. Joel Porte, *The Romance in America: Studies in Cooper, Poe, Hawthorne, Melville, and James* (Middletown, Conn., 1969), p. ix.

2. Essays that represent the most significant exceptions include: Warner Berthoff, "Ambitious Scheme," *Commentary* 44 (October 1967): 110-14; Martin Green, *Re-Appraisals* (New York, 1967); David Hirsch, "Reality, Manners, and Mr. Trilling," *Sewanee Review* 72 (July-September 1964): 420-32; F. R. Leavis, "The Americanness of American Literature," *Anna Karenina and Other Essays* (New York, 1969), pp. 138-51; Richard Poirier, *A World Elsewhere: The Place of Style in American Literature* (New York, 1966); Delmore Schwartz, "The Duchess' Red Shoes," *Partisan Review* 20 (January-February 1953): 55-73.

3. Richard Chase, *The American Novel and its Tradition* (Garden City, 1957), p. xii.

4. The framework I use only takes care of an English language comparison. Given the present situation, such a comparison is a necessary first step, but ideally American fiction should be viewed in much broader terms.

5. Prior to quoting Hazlitt, Professor Ricks asks, "What are the roots that clutch American fiction? Nearly 150 years ago, William Hazlitt seized a gist —or at any rate what an Englishman repeatedly returns to as a gist. No roots, stony rubbish?" Christopher Ricks, "Convulsive Throes," *The New York Review of Books* 17 (July 22, 1971): 12.

6. David Hirsch, "Reality, Manners, and Mr. Trilling," 420.

7. Lionel Trilling, *The Liberal Imagination* (New York, 1950), pp. 199-215, 247-73.

8. Delmore Schwartz, "The Duchess' Red Shoes," 58-9.

9. Ibid., 59-60.

10. Although one might want to add writers to this list, it seems to me impossible to argue that it is in any serious way unrepresentative of the writers who form the major tradition of nineteenth-century American and English fiction.

11. Charles Feidelson, Jr., *Symbolism and American Literature* (Chicago, 1953), p. 186.

12. D. H. Lawrence, *Sons and Lovers* (New York, 1966), p. 420. The relevance of *St. Mawr* to American fiction is discussed by Richard Poirier in *A World Elsewhere*, pp. 40-49. See also Richard Swigg, *Lawrence, Hardy, and American Literature* (New York, 1972).

13. In fairness to Tanner it should be added that he focuses primarily on Emerson, Whitman, and Twain in the nineteenth century. Nonetheless, his

argument is based on the standard generalization that American writers are "too disinclined to develop a complex reaction to society." (Tony Tanner, *The Reign of Wonder: Naivety and Reality in American Literature* [Cambridge, England, 1965], pp. 338-61.)

2

The Failure of Genre Criticism

I   It is tempting to offer a political explanation, albeit one closer to the logic of George Orwell's "Politics and the English Language" than to that of Noam Chomsky's *American Power and the New Mandarins,* for the way the majority of academic critics in the quarter century following World War II have tried to answer the question, What is unique about American fiction?[1] For their inflated view of its distinctiveness, their willingness to ignore qualities it shares with other traditions, so often duplicate the habit of mind that has allowed American political life to escape serious comparative judgment.[2] Yet the critics themselves turn out to have such a diverse set of interests and commitments that any single extra-literary generalization about them is unsatisfactory. If one is serious about proposing an alternative to their theories, he must take on the orthodox task of analyzing their work in relation to the nineteenth-century fiction on which it is based.

The starting point for such an analysis is clear. It is with the theory that has dominated criticism of American fiction for the last twenty-five years: the theory that American fiction is romantic and English fiction is novelistic and that these genres provide a basis for categorizing and distinguishing the two traditions. This view originates in two essays from Lionel Trilling's *The Liberal Imagination,* "Manners, Morals, and the Novel" and "Art and Fortune," receives its most direct expression in Richard Chase's *The American Novel and its Tradi-*

tion, and is implicit in Marius Bewley's *The Eccentric Design.* It is an interpretation of American fiction as romance that rests on two major descriptive points. First, the American writer did not have before him the kind of dense society the English novelist did, and therefore in American fiction, in contrast to English fiction, writers have not used social observation to achieve their profoundest effects but have sought a reality tangential to society.[3] Second, in subject matter and in presentation, American fiction, unlike English fiction, is not bound by the ordinary and veers toward myth, allegory, and symbolism.[4]

The theoretical basis for seeing fiction in these terms is very much in evidence during the nineteenth century in the criticism of writers on both sides of the Atlantic.[5] In his "Essay on Romance," written in 1823 for the *Encyclopedia Britannica,* Sir Walter Scott observed, "We would be rather inclined to describe a Romance as 'a fictitious narrative in prose or verse; the interest of which turns upon marvellous and uncommon incidents;' being thus opposed to the kindred term Novel . . . which we would rather define as 'a fictitious narrative, differing from the Romance because the events are accommodated to the ordinary train of human events and the modern state of society.' "[6] In his preface to *The House of the Seven Gables* Hawthorne used similar language to draw virtually the same distinctions, "When a writer calls his work a Romance, it need hardly be observed that he wishes to claim a certain latitude, both as to its fashion and material, which he would not have thought himself entitled to asume had he professed to be writing a novel."[7]

The debts Trilling, Chase, and Bewley owe to nineteenth-century criticism are, however, minor and not major. In assigning them collective responsibility for the current genre view of American fiction, the only allowance we need make is for the particular emphases and qualifications in their writing. We need not pull back from the assertion that individually and collectively their criticism would have us see American fiction as romantic and English fiction as novelistic.

The particular emphases in Trilling's, Chase's, and Bewley's writing provide a clear case in point. For they reveal nothing so much as similar conclusions arrived at by slightly differing routes. Trilling's primary concern is the relationship between manner and the novel:

> the novel as I have described it has never really established itself in America. . . . the novel in America diverges from its classic intention, which, as I have said, is the investigation of the problem of reality beginning in the social field. The fact is that American writers of genius have not turned their minds to society. Poe and Melville were quite apart from it; the reality they sought was only tangential to society. Hawthorne was acute when he insisted that he did not write novels but romances—he thus expressed his awareness of the lack of social texture in his work.[8]

Richard Chase's basic interest is in "making accurate judgments about what is specifically American in American novels":

> In the first chapter, I try to bring out certain contrasting characteristics of the American novels as opposed to the English, in an attempt to account for the obvious fact that although most of the great American novels are romances, most of the English novels are not —the fact, in other words, that the tradition of romance is major in the history of the American novel but minor in the history of the English novel.[9]

For Marius Bewley, who in the opening chapter of *The Eccentric Design* quotes with approval Trilling's assertion that "the novel as I have described it has never really established itself in America," what is crucial is the connection between social thinness and the "form of life" in American fiction:

> the writers I have dealt with here suggest that life for the serious American artist has a distinctive quality and set of interests of its own, and that these have traditionally been determined and conditioned by the deprivations and confinements of the American condition, and directed by a specific set of problems or tensions growing out of the historical circumstances of America's existence.[10]

The qualifications in Trilling's, Chase's, and Bewley's work are a more complicated matter. Lionel Trilling's statements on the novel and social texture must be considered in light of his essay, "Reality in America," in which he castigates Vernon Parrington for his narrow interpretation of reality in Hawthorne.[11] Richard Chase's willingness to make genre distinctions must be measured against his observation that "we would be pursuing a chimera, if we tried, except provisionally, to isolate a literary form known as the American prose romance, as distinguished from the European or American novel."[12] Marius Bewley's belief in the "eccentric design" of American fiction must be weighed against this conclusion that "we can see what a different breed of artists these American novelists are in their deepest hearts from their European fellows, but how, under their wide diversities, they all bear a resemblance to each other."[13]

Unfortunately, these qualifications by Trilling, Chase, and Bewley are not a practical guide to their work, and, above all, do not account for the way they distinguish American from English fiction. When we read Trilling, we see how it is his belief that in America there was "no opportunity for the novelist to do his job" that defines his analysis. The same pattern, the same negative emphasis, follows in Chase and Bewley. It is the "solitary position" man has been placed in in America that leads Chase to his conclusions about why the romance flourished in America and the novel in England. And it is Bewley's belief that the American writer was "deprived of adequate social density" that causes him to feel so at home with Trilling's view on the inability of the novel to survive in America.

II   Once we are in a position to address ourselves to the genre thesis Trilling, Chase, and Bewley advance without fear of reducing or attenuating it, we come to a far different set of problems. For what remains is a consistent and important view of American fiction in which all three critics fail in their attempt to define its uniqueness. Their essays do not provide an accurate measure—social or aesthetic—of the differences between nineteenth-century American and English fiction. It is clear not only in a very literal way that romantic elements are important to English fiction and novelistic elements are important to American fiction; it is also clear that these qualities are interdependent: that we cannot speak of romantic impulses being so consistently predominant in American fiction and novelistic impulses being so consistently predominant in English fiction that we have a basis for regarding the two traditions (or a wide range of fiction within the two traditions) as different genres.[14]

On a practical level this criticism of the genre approach to American and English fiction becomes much easier to follow. To begin with, although it is true that American writers "did not draw on social observation to achieve their profoundest effects,"[15] it is by no means apparent that most English writers have. In George Eliot's work, for example, the role of society is crucial, but in *The Mill on the Floss*, Maggie Tulliver's decision not to marry Stephen Guest has less to do with society than with her own sense of sacrifice. Similarly, in *Middlemarch* Dorothea Brooke may reject the society into which she was born, but her decision to marry Will Ladislaw depends on her recognition of her own psychological and sexual needs. It would be an equal oversimplification of Dickens to say that social observation explains his profundity as a writer. In *Great Expectations* it is only when Pip realizes that his moral obligations require him to abandon his social ambitions that he achieves maturity, and in *Hard Times* it is Sissy Jupe's instinctive kindness, with its absence of social theory, that triumphs over Gradgrind's utilitarianism. As for Hardy, although social observation is obviously important in his work, it does not by itself reveal the depth or the poetry of his insights. Tess's love of Angel Claire and her murder of Alec D'Urberville are not adequately explained by her social position any more than Jude's unhappy marriage and his premature death are accounted for simply by the snobbery of Christminster.

The same kinds of problems occur if we assume that in nineteenth-century American fiction social observation is a "tangential" matter: that "American writers of genius have not turned their minds to society" and that they have a tendency "to ignore the spectacle of man in society."[16] We must blind ourselves not only to the overt concern with society in books like *The Blithedale Romance* and *The Gilded Age*, we must also ignore subtler and equally important social questions. Yet it is difficult to imagine the Leatherstocking Tales without Cooper's theories on the growth of nations. There would be no dramatic tension in *The Pioneers* if it were not for Natty's conflict with the system of law and order Judge Temple asserts must govern the settlements, and *The Prairie* would not be nearly so significant without Natty's conflict with the spirit of frontier ruthlessness that Ishmael Bush represents. In Hawthorne's work social considerations are no less important. In *The Scarlet Letter* the Puritan community is an active force against which Hester strives and before which Dimmesdale confesses. Without the community the questions of guilt and innocence that Hawthorne raises would not be brought into focus so dramatically or so completely.[17]

Indeed, even when we reduce the question of social observation to the narrower question of class and status, it is not apparent that the differences between American and English fiction are as pervasive or as substantive as the genre critics indicate or that "the American novelist before James, in his most successful work, turns his back on manners and society as such."[18] To say this is not to go as far as Quentin Anderson does in *The Imperial Self* when he asserts, "There is no essential difference between Jane Austen's exquisitely modulated use of the marital maneuvers of country squires and Hawthorne's use of the Puritan ethos. These were the available traditions."[19] But it is to insist on two other points. First, as Cooper's Effinghams, Hawthorne's Pyncheons, and Melville's Glendinnings show, the American writer was responsive to the significance of class and status. Secondly, for English writers like Eliot and Dickens, class and status were frequently of secondary rather than of primary interest. In *Adam Bede* it is the moral deadness of so much of village life, not simply the traditional divisions of class, that separates people from one another, and in *Hard Times* it is the mechanical nature of human relationships—a failing that cuts across class lines and has more to do with the nature of industrialism than with social stratification—that causes the greatest suffering.

The same kinds of weaknesses also appear in the argument that American fiction is not bound by the ordinary, that, in Richard Chase's words, it has "an assumed freedom from the ordinary novelistic requirements of verisimilitude."[20] When we think of certain works of Hawthorne and Melville, this argument seems valid. Yet as soon as we go beyond this perspective, the argument begins to develop flaws. For example, in their metaphysical and psychological concerns, Melville and Hardy have more in common than Melville and Cooper. With its terrors and theological implications, the universe of Ahab and Pierre comes nearer that of Tess and Jude than that of Natty and Chingachgook. Moreover, if freedom from the ordinary means freedom from the usual, then Scott and Dickens qualify as Americans in a number of ways. Rob Roy's miraculous escapes and appearances have as little to do with the probable as Krook's death by "spontaneous combustion" in *Bleak House,* and despite all that we know, about a figure like Quilp or Miss Havishman, neither is believable as an everyday person. These problems also remain if we take freedom from the ordinary to mean technique rather than subject matter. By this criterion there is nothing English about Thomas Hardy with his highly stylized writing, his maneuverings of plot, and his heavy-handed ironies.

Finally, it is impossible to accept as adequate the genre assertion that American fiction is distinguishable because it veers, "more freely" than English fiction, "toward mythic, allegorical, and symbolistic forms."[21] Too much is left out by such a description. It does not reflect how the kind of allegory in Hawthorne's and Melville's fiction has no real parallel, say, in the work of Cooper,[22] nor does it account for the importance of myth and symbolism in nineteenth-century English fiction. Yet Highland myth is essential to Scott's Waverly novels, and folk myth, as well as biblical and Greek myth, are vital to Hardy's Wessex novels. As for symbolism, it is an integral part of Dickens' writing (the fog in *Bleak House,* the river in *Great Expectations*) and crucial to the major scenes in Eliot's novels (the fragments of machinery in *The Mill on the Floss,* the storm and lightning in *Middlemarch*). The question needing to be asked in all these cases is: How are myth and symbolism different in American fiction and in English fiction? For example, how do they show us that Hawthorne and Twain are closer than Dickens and Twain, that American fiction is actually a different kind of fiction from English fiction? These are questions genre criticism never comes to terms with. It does not distinguish between a timeless symbol and one that is limited by history or between a myth that provides an epic framework and one that provides a cultural backdrop, and so in the end it reveals only the outward form that style takes in nineteenth-century American fiction.

III   By themselves these descriptive
failings are sufficient to disqualify genre criticism as a critical guide
to the uniqueness of American fiction. But what makes them especially serious is that they stem from a series of methodological
errors underlying not only genre criticism but those studies of
American fiction which, by virtue of qualities they share or derive
from genre criticism, may be regarded as variants of it: for example,
Charles Feidelson's *Symbolism and American Literature,* Leslie Fiedler's
Love and Death in the American Novel, Edwin Fussell's *Frontier,* Daniel
Hoffman's *Form and Fable in American Fiction,* Harry Levin's *The Power
of Blackness,* R. W. B. Lewis's *The American Adam,* Leo Marx's *The
Machine in the Garden,* and Joel Porte's *The Romance in America.*[23]
Warner Berthoff has classified such books as interpretative essays
that ignore parallels, inflate limited evidence, and find organic uni-
ties in American fiction where often none exist.[24] But Professor
Berthoff's criticisms do not go far enough in explaining how books
containing such breadth of purpose and intelligence can provide so
misleading an account of the uniqueness of American fiction.[25]
(Here it is necessary to emphasize that my attack on these books is
directed only toward the single question of uniqueness. It does not
offer anything like a full-scale review of them, nor does it represent
an attempt to dismiss the insights they provide on matters ranging
from the "westering" myth to the folklore tradition in American
fiction.)

To come to terms with the methodological errors underlying
genre criticism and its variants, it is necessary to deal with at least
three specific points of confusion:

1) *The characteristic for the unique:* It is commonplace to argue that
what characterizes American fiction distinguishes it. Yet it is equally
clear that what characterizes American fiction may characterize
other literature and that genre criticism sets a pattern for ignoring
this problem when it fails at a practical level to treat American and
English fiction as mixed or hybrid strains. How serious this kind of
comparative oversight can be is apparent from the fact that even so
brilliant a study as R. W. B. Lewis's *The American Adam* is a misleading guide to the uniqueness of nineteenth-century American fiction.
Although Professor Lewis's analysis reveals the importance of the

Adamic figure in American literature, it does not (as its title suggests) show how there is a uniquely American Adam. By ignoring parallels, it provides no way of coping with the problem that in English fiction the Adamic figure is not only explicitly recalled in George Eliot's *Adam Bede* but implicitly recalled in a number of other works. This general use of the Adamic type is apparent even when one takes only a single definition of the American Adam employed by Professor Lewis: "the young innocent, liberated from family and social history or bereft of them; advancing hopefully into a complex world he knows not of . . . defeated, perhaps even destroyed."[26] Such a definition clearly fits Eliot's Will Ladislaw, Thackeray's Henry Esmond, and Hardy's Jude Fawley.

2) *The specific for the unique:* This view is based on the idea that if one finds a particular concern, for example, a mythic interest in the Garden of Eden, indigenous to American fiction and absent from English fiction, he is in a position to generalize about the distinctiveness of American fiction. This theory has its origins in the corollary to the genre argument that manners and class tensions reveal the nature of the English novel: the corollary being that typically American concerns reveal the nature of American fiction. In practice the specific fallacy misleads as much by what it fails to say as by what it says. Edwin Fussell's painstakingly careful study in *Frontier* of American literature and the American West provides a case in point. Professor Fussell's thesis is that "for an understanding of early American literature, the word West, with all its derivatives and variants, is the all but inevitable key."[27] But unless subject matter is to be equated with angle and shape of vision, such a key is at best an index to one kind of concern in American fiction. It is not a common denominator that unites or eliminates more important factors or by its presence distinguishes one literary form from another.[28]

3) *The pervasive for the unique:* This theory works on the assumption that a concern not textually paramount in any particular novel can, by virtue of its inherent significance and presence throughout a number of novels, reveal the uniqueness of American fiction. Genre criticism, which so often analyzes parts of books independently of their full text, encourages this kind of theorizing, which at its most

complicated level is reflected in Leslie Fiedler's *Love and Death in the American Novel*. Professor Fiedler argues that American fiction is distinguishable by its failure to deal with "adult heterosexual love,"[29] and as proof of this assertion he cites, among other examples, the asceticism of Natty Bumppo, the frustration of Hester Prynne, and the closeness of Huck and Jim. The difficulty with Professor Fiedler's thesis is not that his argument on the nature of sexuality in American fiction is wrong, but that he is writing about fiction in which sexual psychology does not explain as much about literary form or the behavior of individuals as do other matters: spatial freedom in Cooper, original sin in Hawthorne, egalitarianism in Twain. Thus in order to use Professor Fiedler's thesis to distinguish nineteenth-century American fiction, we must accept the idea that it is possible to explain the uniqueness of a fictional tradition while ignoring its overriding metaphorical and thematic concerns.

These three fallacies do not reveal all that is descriptively wrong with genre criticism and its variants, nor is it necessary that they should. It is enough that alone or in combination they are at the root of virtually every important error and account for the fact that, in trying to describe uniqueness, genre criticism and its variants have postulated either a superform in which American fiction is depicted as a combination of qualities (which are not true for any one book and have no viable organizing principle) or a fragmented form in which single qualities are said to reveal the essence of American fiction (despite the fact that other qualities are often of equal or greater importance).

IV   The descriptive failings of genre criticism and its variants are not isolated phenomena, however. They are directly related to the historical theories genre criticism has used to explain the uniqueness of Americn fiction and to the modifications of these theories the variants of genre criticism have employed. At the root of both approaches is the belief that the explanation for the uniqueness of American fiction is to be found in the conditions out of which it grew rather than in the fiction itself.

Overlooked is the distinction between writing history and writing a novel made by R.G. Collingwood in *The Idea of History,* "Where they do differ is that the historian's picture is meant to be true. The novelist has a single task only: to construct a coherent picture, one that makes sense. The historian has a double task: he has both to do this, and to construct a picture of things . . . as they really happened."[30] In contrast to Collingwood, the genre critics and those whom they have influenced assume a causal relationship between history and literature that borders on determinism.

The nineteenth-century version of this relationship appears most prominently in Tocqueville's *Democracy in America,* "I should say more than I mean if I were to assert that the literature of a nation is always subordinate to its social state and political constitution. I am aware that, independently of these causes, there are several others which confer certain characteristics on literary productions; but these appear to me to be the chief."[31] The connection that Tocqueville draws between American history and American literature depends upon two observations. The first is the general observation that in democratic nations writers have a taste for "abstract expressions" and a need to describe "man himself taken aloof from his country and his age."[32] The second is the specific observation that in America literary conditions are the product of two related forces: the dullness of a society without rank or tradition and the vitality of a national ethos. "Nothing conceivable is so petty, so insipid, so crowded with paltry interests—in one word, so anti-poetic—as the life of a man in the United States," Tocqueville notes, and then adds, "But among the thoughts which it suggests, there is always one that is full of poetry, and that is the hidden nerve which gives vigor to the whole frame."[33] The thought "full of poetry" that Tocqueville has in mind is the American march across the wilderness, a "magnificent image" that continues to haunt every American "in his least as well as in his most important actions." Tocqueville's analysis does not become more detailed because he believed that "properly speaking" America had "no literature"—only "journalists."[34] But it is a short transition from his kind of theorizing about American literature to that which is still prevalent. How short a transition it is can be seen by examining four assertions that explicitly characterize genre criticism and implicitly (albeit less uniformly) characterize its variants.

1) *The English novel did not survive in America because the texture of American society was too thin to support such an art form:* This view has its origins in Lionel Trilling's assertion in *The Liberal Imagination,* "In this country the real basis of the novel has never existed—that is, the tension between a middle class and an aristocracy which brings manners into observable relief as the living representation of ideals and the living comment on ideas."[35] Trilling's views on what the absence of a traditional class structure means are amplified by Marius Bewley in *The Eccentric Design:*

> But the American novelist had only his *ideas* with which to begin: ideas which, for the most part, were grounded in the great American democratic abstractions. And he found that these abstractions were disembodied, that there was no social context in which they might acquire a rich human relevance. For the traditional novelist, the universal and the particular come together in the world of manners; but for the American artist there was no social surface responsive to his touch.[36]

The assumption underlying these statements is that in only one kind of historical situation will a writer look closely at society and find enough value in it to produce "traditional" novels. But what is confused is an attitude toward society and society itself. To assume that because he lacked a socially thick environment the American writer was forced to turn away from society and to abandon the English novel form is to ignore all the other reasons he had for writing the way he did. It is also to overlook the more obvious fact that a writer like Henry James was able to describe American society with the detail of an English novelist, and that Hawthorne, when he lived and worked in Europe, continued to describe European society as he did American society.

2) *The thinness of American society accounts not only for the absence of the English novel in America but provides a basic explanation for the form of American fiction:* To quote Marius Bewley again, "The absence of a traditional social medium in America compelled the original American artist to confront starkly his own emotional and spiritual needs

which his art then became the means of comprehending and analys-
ing."[37] In critical practice this statement means that social thinness
sets into play forces that produce the American rather than the
English novel. Yet it is impossible to apply this statement with any
consistency or to find a good theoretical justification for it. Certainly
it does not work out in terms of genre. The prose romance that
Richard Chase finds so characteristic of American fiction did not
flourish in the nineteenth century where life in the United States was
thinnest. There the stark prose of Hamlin Garland and Edward
Eggleston was dominant. Similarly, in Britain a socially active Sir
Walter Scott was able to develop his romances out of a vivid sense
of past and present tradition, and Emily Brontë had no difficulty in
ignoring most of the literary and social conventions around her and
extending the development of the gothic romance. The problem
gets even worse if one tries to update such a view. For it is difficult
to see how social thinness can account for the form of American
fiction after World War I. Yet most of the thin-soil critics claim that
the American fictional tradition continues beyond this period.

   3) *The historical uniqueness of America accounts for the uniqueness of
American fiction:* This view can occur as either a reversal or an extension of the negative historical explanations of American fiction, but
when combined with a sense of English and American history, it has
none of their obvious failings. The following passage from *The
Eccentric Design* provides a case in point:

> But the writers I have dealt with here suggest that 'life' for the serious
> American artist has a distinctive quality and set of interests of its own,
> and that these have traditionally been determined and conditioned by
> the deprivations and confinements of the American condition, and di-
> rected by a specific set of problems or tensions growing out of the
> historical circumstances of America's existence. Obviously no generaliza-
> tions can be offered that will apply equally to all the novelists treated
> here, nor even to as many as two of them in the same way. But this much,
> at least, is worth hazarding: the novelists treated here are, as a group,
> extraordinarily non-sensuous. . . . Because the American tradition pro-
> vided its artists with abstractions and ideas rather than with manners, we
> have no great characters, but great symbolic personifications and mythic
> embodiments that go under the names of Natty Bumppo, Jay Gatsby,

Huckleberry Finn, Ahab, Ishmael—all of whom are strangely unrelated
to the world of ordinary passions and longings, for the democrat is at last
the loneliest man in the universe.[38]

One can dispute various contentions in such a passage, but its
ultimate weaknesses become apparent only when the whole concep-
tual value of historical explanations for the uniqueness of American
fiction is questioned. To insist that such explanations are misleading when they take the kind of expansive form discussed here is not,
of course, to maintain that American fiction in the nineteenth century was idiosyncratic or ahistorical. It is instead to argue that,
although the form of American fiction often grew out of a response
to American history, knowing the historical situation does not provide a causal explanation for the literary form. It provides an explanation only for one of several influences with which the form deals.
In order to establish a direct connection between history and a
literary form (or even the life within a literary form), it is necessary
to remember that we are moving between two different realms and
that the given conditions of the first are not automatically the imag-
ined conditions of the second. Therefore, showing causality requires either knowledge that a particular set of historical circumstances inevitably leads to a particular literary result or relatively
complete understanding of the point where a writer's imagination
ends and his thought is imposed by his environment. Take away
these conditions, as we must when analyzing nineteenth-century
American fiction, and what remains to be said is important, but it
reveals only cultural parallels and influences.

4) *The complaints of American writers against American society are evidence
that the texture of American society forced them to write romances rather than
novels:* This line of reasoning is pursued by Lionel Trilling in *The
Liberal Imagination.* After citing the passages in James's life of Hawthorne in which James enumerates all that is missing from American
society, Trilling concludes:

That is, no sufficiency of means . . . no opportunity for the novelist to
do his job of searching out reality, not enough complication of appearance to make the job interesting. Another great American novelist of very

different temperament had said much the same thing decades before: James Fenimore Cooper found that American manners were too simple and dull to nourish the novelist.[39]

The shortcomings of such an interpretation of Cooper or Hawthorne or James become apparent when one looks closely at their specific complaints about America, which do not yield the conclusion that in this country the novel was uniquely difficult to write. In Cooper's *Notions of the Americans* all forms of writing are judged difficult to accomplish in the United States:

> The second obstacle against which American literature has to contend is in the poverty of the materials. . . . There are no annals for the historian; no follies (beyond the most vulgar and commonplace) for the satirist; no manners for the dramatist; no obscure fictions for the writer of romance; no gross and hardy offences against decorum for the moralist; nor any of the rich artificial auxiliaries of poetry.[40]

Similarly, in his preface to *The Marble Faun* Hawthorne is not maintaining, as Richard Chase claims he is, "that romance, rather than the novel, was the predestined form of American narrative."[41] To the contrary, what is especially revealing about Hawthorne's *Marble Faun* preface is his assertion of how difficult it is to write a romance in America, "No author, without a trial, can conceive of the difficulty or writing a romance about a country where there is no shadow, no antiquity, no picturesque and gloomy wrong . . . as is happily the case with my dear native land."[42] Indeed, even Henry James in his study of Hawthorne is not arguing that Hawthorne or the American writer was forced to create romances rather than novels. Early in the biography James specifically observes that the uses a writer makes of a provincial environment are "relative" and depend on his "point of view," and on the same page as his list of complaints about all that is "absent in the texture of American life," he comments that the feeling one gets on imagining Hawthorne's surroundings "is that of compassion for a romancer looking for subjects in such a field."[43]

V   Once we are beyond the limitations of genre criticism and its variants, what can be said about the
uniqueness of nineteenth-century American fiction makes sense
only if two conditions are met: American fiction is analyzed in comparison with rather than in isolation from English fiction, and the
question of form in American fiction is treated in its full dimension.

The most obvious and important value of a comparative analysis
of nineteenth-century American and English fiction is that it puts
the two traditions in perspective, creating a situation in which what
is said about the one can be tested against the other. Without this
kind of critical possibility the question of uniqueness in nineteenth-
century American fiction cannot be answered.[44] It can merely be
approached from a well-reasoned but isolated point of view. If properly used, a comparative analysis also guarantees that the differences between writers like Melville and Jane Austen will not serve
as the basis for generalizations about American fiction. This is not
to say a comparison of Melville and Austen may not be of value but
that it raises further problems: Are not many of the differences
between Melville and Austen, like many of those between Hardy and
Austen, explicable by their relative positions within a literary tradition? Is this distinction not as important as the factor that they
represent different traditions? Are not the conclusions that can be
drawn about such disparate writers far too broad to include writers
as similar as Scott and Cooper? These questions need to be asked,
but they can be settled only when a comparison of American and
English fiction analyzes the two traditions at the points at which they
are closest, e.g., in the work of Scott and Cooper or Melville and
Hardy. Any less tightly drawn comparison will not stand up as a
generalization.

The same kinds of problems make it necessary to treat the question of form in American fiction in terms of its overall effect. Too
often in the past the uniqueness of American fiction has been
defined on the basis of only one aspect of form, for example symbolism; or else so-called distinguishing elements in American fiction,
like myth and allegory, have been studied independently of the
larger context in which they appear. Overlooked has been the fact
that the novel cannot, as Philip Rahv observes in *The Myth and the*

Powerhouse, "accommodate a declaration of independence by the smaller unit" but must rely on the cumulative effect of a number of elements: style, plot, subject matter, inventiveness.[45]

The value of approaching form in this way can be seen with special clarity if we put the problem of defining the uniqueness of American fiction into architectural terms and substitute the idea of a building for that of a book. Knowing the location of the building, the materials from which it is constructed, and its intended purpose still leaves a vague picture of the structure. We may realize the building will be glass and steel and contain offices rather than apartments, but we do not know its actual shape or what peculiar significance it may acquire. In the case of a book of fiction, knowing plot, style, and subject matter (or a much broader range of elements) does not in itself provide an adequate picture of form or of meaning. We need to understand much more; at the very least, the relationship and cumulative effect of all the elements comprising the text in question.[46]

The point to which this analogy returns is that a broad, comparative analysis has the capacity to reveal, as genre criticism and its variants do not, the uniqueness and the complexity of nineteenth-century American fiction. Stated as a general proposition, what this comes down to is:

1) Distinguishing American from English fiction requires analysis of the total process by which certain qualities common to both traditions are given unique emphasis in one or the other tradition.

2) The most accurate measure of the difference between the two traditions is reflected in two facts:

   a) Nineteenth-century American fiction gives an ultimate importance (and textual dominance) to certain ideational or visionary concerns that finally makes these concerns superior to or situationally transcendent of the social context in which they appear.

   b) Nineteenth-century English fiction gives a qualified importance (and textual limitation) to such concerns that finally makes them coextensive with or subordinate to the social context in which they appear.

The picture of nineteenth-century American and English fiction that this definition yields is one in which the differences between the two traditions can be likened to the differences between a spire and a dome, both of which have a solid foundation but each of which has a different sweep—that of the spire sending it above and then beyond its source; that of the dome sending it above and back to its source.

The task of the next five chapters is to try to make explicit this general proposition and to put in final perspective the ways in which the view of American fiction advanced here differs from that advanced by the genre critics and those whom they have influenced.

NOTES

1. George Orwell, "Politics and the English Language," *A Collection of Essays* (Garden City, 1954), pp. 162–77; Noam Chomsky, *American Power and the New Mandarins* (New York, 1969). See also Mark L. Krupnick, "Lionel Trilling: Criticism and Illusion," *Modern Occasions* 1 (Winter 1971): 282–7.

2. For a more detailed treatment of how recent analyses of American literature "suffer as a class from the same feelings that have afflicted American politics, on all sides, for the past twenty years," see Warner Berthoff, "Ambitious Scheme," *Commentary* 44 (October 1967): 111. Richard Bridgman reviews the historic relationship between nationalism and the wish, on the part of criticism, for a national literature in *The Colloquial Style in America* (New York, 1966), pp. 7–43.

3. Trilling regards James's list of all that was missing in American life as proof that in this country there was "no opportunity for the novelist to do his job of searching out reality, not enough complication of appearance to make the job interesting." On the same page he also says of Poe and Melville: "the reality they sought was only tangential to society." He then expands upon his statement to argue, "In America in the nineteenth century, Henry James was alone in knowing that to scale the moral and aesthetic heights in the novel one had to use the ladder of social observation." ("Manners, Morals, and the Novel," *The Liberal Imagination*, p. 206.) Chase speaks of "the solitary position man has been placed in this country, a position very early enforced by the doctrines of Puritanism and later by frontier conditions," as one of the "historical facts" which have "vivified and excited the American imagination." He then asserts, "Romance does

not plant itself, like the novel, solidly in the midst of the actual." (*The American Novel and its Tradition*, pp. 11, 19.) Bewley writes, "The traditional codes and manners by which the European novelist creates his men and women were not at his [the American author's] disposal. . . . the most significant American novelists before Henry James . . . did not draw on social observation to achieve their profoundest effects"; indeed, "for the American artist there was no social surface responsive to his touch." (*The Eccentric Design* [New York, 1963], pp. 14, 15.)

4. Trilling speaks of American novels providing "few substantial or memorable people. . . . The great characters of American fiction . . . tend to be mythic." ("Art and Fortune," *The Liberal Imagination*, p. 254.) Richard Chase speaks of the romance having an "assumed freedom from the ordinary novelistic requirements of verisimilitude," and later observes, "Being less committed to the immediate rendition of reality than the novel, the romance will more freely veer toward mythic, allegorical, and symbolistic forms." (*The American Novel and its Tradition*, pp. ix, 13.) Marius Bewley emphasizes how in American fiction there is "so little leafage of shared manners, inherited institutions, and traditional attitudes." He concludes by observing that in American fiction "we have no great characters, but great symbolic personifications and mythic embodiments. . . . James's famous list of all the American novelists did not possess in the way of subject matter is, in the end, a description of those conditions that gave rise to symbolism in American art." (*The Eccentric Design*, pp. 290, 293–4.)

5. The modern extension of this theoretical view is to be found in Northrop Frye's observation, "The romancer does not attempt to create 'real people' so much as stylized figures which expand into psychological archetypes. . . . The novelist deals with . . . characters wearing their *personae* or social masks. He needs the framework of a stable society, and many of our best novelists have been conventional to the verge of fussiness. The romancer deals with individuality, with characters *in vacuo* idealized by revery. . . ." (*Anatomy of Criticism* [Princeton, 1957], pp. 304–305.)

6. Walter Scott, "Essay on Romance," *The Miscellaneous Prose Works*, 6 (Edinburgh, 1834), p. 129.

7. Nathaniel Hawthorne, *The House of the Seven Gables* (Columbus, Ohio, 1965), p. 1.

8. Lionel Trilling, "Manners, Morals, and the Novel," *The Liberal Imagination*, p. 206.

9. Richard Chase, *The American Novel and its Tradition*, p. xii.

10. Marius Bewley, *The Eccentric Design*, pp. 292–3.

11. Lionel Trilling, "Reality in America," *The Liberal Imagination*, p. 7.

12. Richard Chase, *The American Novel and its Tradition*, p. 14. It is interesting to note that Chase also observes, "In actuality the romances are literary hybrids, unique only in their peculiar but widely differing amalgamation of

novelistic and romance elements." What Chase does not do is suggest that the English novel is also a hybrid. Thus, his real comparison is between American and English romances, not novels. This is consistent with the thrust of his book, which has the "romance elements" of American fiction providing its real definition.

13. Marius Bewley, *The Eccentric Design*, p. 294.

14. More often than not, and especially in practical analysis, Trilling, Chase, and Bewley are rigid in their insistence that romantic elements are vital to American fiction and novelistic or societal concerns are not. Trilling makes the blanket statement, "American writers of genius have not turned their minds to society." ("Manners, Morals, and the Novel," p. 206.) Chase speaks of the tendency of romance "to ignore the spectacle of man in society." (*The American Novel and its Tradition*, p. ix.) Bewley asserts that "for the American artist there was no social surface responsive to his touch." (*The Eccentric Design*, p. 15.)

15. Marius Bewley, *The Eccentric Design*, p. 14.

16. Lionel Trilling, "Manners, Morals, and the Novel," p. 206. Richard Chase, *The American Novel and its Tradition*, p. ix.

17. As Alan Heimert has shown, even in *Moby Dick* social and political anaylsis is crucial. "*Moby Dick* and American Political Symbolism," *American Quarterly* 15 (Fall 1963): 498–534.

18. Marius Bewley, *The Eccentric Design*, p. 15.

19. Quentin Anderson, *The Imperial Self* (New York, 1971), p. 78.

20. Richard Chase, *The American Novel and its Tradition*, p. ix.

21. Ibid., p. 13.

22. In *Dark Conceit: The Making of Allegory* (New York, 1966), the only American writers Edwin Honig speaks of in detail are Hawthorne and Melville. Honig's study is particularly thorough, and therefore his omission of writers like Cooper and Twain is especially significant for what it says about the extent of allegory in nineteenth-century American fiction.

23. The books that I classify as variants of genre criticism all make claims for the uniqueness of nineteenth-century American fiction that cannot bear comparative scrutiny or do not adequately explain the nature and variety of American fiction in this period. They are related to genre criticism in that they incorporate one or more of the following genre assertions: American fiction is free from the ordinary and can be distinguished in terms of certain technical qualities, for example, myth or symbolism. The American writer was at best tangentially interested in society. Separateness from Europe, as a negative fact of cultural deprivation or a positive fact of a new experience, is sufficient to account for the uniqueness of American fiction. This list of books is by no means exhaustive, nor does it include relevant collections of shorter essays, such as Perry Miller's *Nature's Nation* (Cambridge, Mass., 1967).

24. Warner Berthoff, "Ambitious Scheme," 110–14.

25. For an alternative approach to the romance in America see Tony Tanner, "Notes for a Comparison Between American and European Romanticism," *Journal of American Studies* (April 1968): 83–103.

26. R. W. B. Lewis, *The American Adam* (Chicago, 1961), p. 127–8.

27. Edwin Fussell, *Frontier* (Princeton, 1965), p. 3.

28. For an attack on history that overemphasizes the "native" factor of the frontier see Louis Hartz, *The Founding of New Societies* (New York, 1964), pp. 10, 69–70.

29. Leslie Fiedler, *Love and Death in the American Novel* (New York, 1966), pp. 12–13.

30. R. G. Collingwood, *The Idea of History* (New York, 1967), p. 246.

31. Alexis de Tocqueville, *Democracy in America*, II, ed. Phillips Bradley (New York, 1958), p. 63.

32. Ibid., pp. 73, 81.

33. Ibid., pp. 78–9.

34. Ibid., pp. 78, 59.

35. Lionel Trilling, "Art and Fortune," p. 252.

36. Marius Bewley, *The Eccentric Design*, p. 15.

37. Ibid., p. 19.

38. Ibid., pp. 292–3.

39. Lionel Trilling, "Manners, Morals, and the Novel," p. 206.

40. James Fenimore Cooper, *The Travelling Bachelor or Notions of the Americans*, vol. 2 (New York, 1852), p. 108.

41. Richard Chase, *The American Novel and its Tradition*, p. 18.

42. Nathaniel Hawthorne, *The Marble Faun* (Columbus, 1968), p. 3.

43. Henry James, *Hawthorne* (Ithaca, 1956), pp. 10, 34.

44. It is obvious that American fiction can be distinguished from French or Russian or German fiction in terms of language. This knowledge is not possible with American and English fiction and so a comparative understanding of the two is a primary necessity.

45. Philip Rahv, *The Myth and the Powerhouse* (New York, 1966), p. 53.

46. See René Wellek, *Concepts of Criticism* (New Haven, 1964), p. 294.

3

$\mathcal{S}$ir Walter Scott and Fenimore Cooper

I To Fenimore Cooper being called the "American Scott" was more than an annoyance.[1] It was a title that provoked him deeply enough to write letters like the following one to Samuel Carter Hall:

> In a note you call me the "rival" of Sir Walter Scott—Now the idea of rivalry with him never crossed my brain. I have always spoken, written and thought of Sir Walter Scott (as a writer) just as I should think and speak of Shakespeare—with high admiration of his talent, but with no silly reserve, as if my own position rendered it necessary that I should use more delicacy than other men. . . . If there is a term that gives me more disgust than any other, it is to be called, as some on the continent *advertise* me, the "American Walter Scott."[2]

Cooper's letter to Hall is not without a basis, however. As one of his earliest biographers, Thomas R. Lounsbury, observed in a study written in 1882, "To call Cooper the American Scott in compliment in the days of his popularity and in derision in the days of his unpopularity, was a method of criticism which enabled men to praise or undervalue without taking the trouble to think."[3] For the twentieth-century reader the danger of Cooper's complaint and Lounsbury's warning is that they stress only the negative side of a Scott–Cooper comparison. They fail to touch upon the ways in which a comparison of the two reveals not only the obvious similarities in their language, their characters, and their fascination with the wilderness, but the underlying unity of their work.[4]

The nature of this unity (which even recent comparisons of Scott and Cooper do not explore in systematic fashion) is reflected in the opening chapter of David Levin's *History as Romantic Art,* in which the romantic historians of nineteenth-century America—Bancroft, Prescott, Motley, and Parkman—are compared with Scott and Cooper:

> Like Cooper and Scott, they were interested in generalizing about such subjects as "national character," and in illustrating through minor characters such abstracted traits as "remarkable resolution," "intrepidity" (especially the intrepidity of an occasional woman), and chivalric generosity. They seemed pleased, too, to be able to show at times that a genuine historical character resembled the fictitious creations of a Scott or a Cooper.[5]

Levin's observations, which have a parallel with observations made by Donald Davie and George Dekkar in their comparisons of Scott and Cooper,[6] point to the fact that if the latter are to be understood in perspective, their historical vision must be seen as playing not only a vital role in their fiction but forming its very structure.

This interpretation of Scott and Cooper is especially appropriate to two of their most popular works, *Rob Roy* and *The Prairie.* Read without an awareness of their historical dimension, *Rob Roy* and *The Prairie* become vulnerable to the kind of satiric attack that Mark Twain levelled against Scott in *Life on the Mississippi* and against Cooper in "Fenimore Cooper's Literary Offenses."[7] On the other hand, when their historical dimension is understood, *Rob Roy* and *The Prairie* assume an entirely different artistic and intellectual significance—one in which their development reflects the tension between two opposed ways of life: the first, a timeless and visibly heroic one in which nature is important and the largest social unit is the clan or the tribe; the second, a new and relatively cautious one in which progress is essential and money and the state are the primary forces.

II   The first of these ways of life is represented by Rob and Natty. It is a form of wilderness existence that on the surface has such a facile and romantic appeal that it is necessary to examine closely Leslie Fiedler's charge that Rob Roy or Natty Bumppo, Robin Hood or Chingachgook "project the bourgeois's own slight margin of resentment against the safe, commercial way of life" and reflect the tribute that philistinism pays to the instinctive, the civilized to the natural.[8] "Scott would not, of course, have wanted to leave Abbotsford for a medieval castle or a Highland hideaway, any more than Cooper would have wanted to abandon his Westchester County home or his Paris hotel for a wigwam; they felt free to create fantasies of flight from civilized comfort to primitive simplicity because they were sure that no one would believe them any more than they believed themselves."[9] The further one reads in *Rob Roy* and *The Prairie*, the more apparent it becomes that Fiedler's analysis distorts the vision of the wilderness presented in both books.

To begin with, the ominousness of the wilderness in which Rob and Natty roam is as important as its so-called "primitive simplicity." In neither book is nature seen from a purely Emersonian perspective. When Scott's narrator leaves Glasgow, it is the barrenness around him that he notices:

> Huge continuous heaths spread before, behind, and around us in hopeless barrenness. . . . There were neither trees nor bushes to relieve the eye from the russet livery of absolute sterility. . . . The very birds seemed to shun these wastes, and no wonder, since they had an easy method of escaping from them. . . . (258)[10]

Cooper uses similar language to describe the prairie, speaking of it as a "bleak and solitary" land with "deep morasses and arid wastes" (4):[11]

> In the little valleys . . . the meagre prospect ran off in long, narrow, barren perspectives, but slightly relieved by a pitiful show of coarse though somewhat luxuriant vegetation. From the summits of the swells, the eye became fatigued with the sameness and chilling dreariness of the landscape. (6)

An equal lack of "bourgeois" picturesqueness applies to Rob's and Natty's reasons for remaining apart from conventional society. Unlike Melville's Polynesian Islanders, the latter are not living in isolation because they have never known society, but because they have fled it. Each has had a humiliating experience with the law that has made it impossible for him to continue his former way of life. In Rob's case he has been victimized by creditors, who, in his words, have left him, "bankrupt, barefooted,—stripped of all, dishonoured and hunted down, because the avarice of others grasped at more than . . . [he] could pay" (350).

This view is one that Bailie Nicol Jarvie (the most reliable figure in Scott's novel on the subject of financial matters) also supports. The Bailie characterizes the treatment of Rob as shameful, asserting that even some of Rob's neighbors "grippit to his living and land" (246). "Rob came hame, and fand desolation . . . where he left plenty; he looked east, west, south, north, and saw neither hauld nor hope" (246). A parallel situation exists in *The Prairie* with regard to Natty's flight from "the States on the sea-shore" (66) and his no less humiliating encounter with authority (described in detail in *The Pioneers*). In his case it is also a naive understanding of societal rules that causes his undoing (he is charged with shooting a deer out of season) and friends who are among those contributing to his downfall (he is sentenced by a judge whose daughter he saved from a "panther"). Finally, like Rob, it is Natty who is best able to describe the shock of his experience:

> "I was carried into one of the lawless holes [jail] myself once, and it was about a thing of no more value than the skin of a deer. . . . it was a solemn sight to see an aged man, who had always lived in the air, laid neck and heels by the law, and held up as a spectacle for the women and boys of a wasteful settlement to point their fingers at!" (377)

The most telling proof of the seriousness, rather than the sentimentality, with which Rob and Natty are treated is, however, to be found in the three factors that provide the clearest explanation for their way of life: the exploitive nature of the society they have fled, the intensely personal sense of honor they uphold, and the spatial vision they believe in.

The exploitive qualities of organized society in *Rob Roy* and *The Prairie* are, indeed, so conspicuous that writers like Georg Lukacs and Maxim Gorky have not been hesitant to attempt a Marxist reading of Scott and Cooper.[12] In *Rob Roy,* although there is no direct connection between Rob's financial troubles and the Act of Union that brought England and Scotland together, it is clear that union works against Rob and those like him.[13] The law in *Rob Roy* is the servant of national and economic interests. Rob is justified in blaming much of the poverty around him on the fact that "English gaugers and supervisors . . . have taen up the trade of thievery over the heads of the native professors" (30–1). Trevelyan asserts as much in his study of *The Peace and the Protestant Succession* when he notes that "in Scotland the first economic consequences of union gave rise to grave and very excusable discontent."[14] And in Scott's novel the English-born Frank Osbaldistone corroborates Rob's view, "The Union had, indeed, opened to Scotland the trade of the English colonies; but betwixt want of capital, and the national jealousy of the English, the merchants of Scotland were as yet excluded . . . from the exericse of privileges which that memorable treaty conferred on them" (179). Frank also gets a first-hand chance to see, as Rob has claimed, that English law is unfairly administered. When he and Nicol Jarvie are suspected of being Scottish outlaws, they are detained by a Captain who informs them that, if they were " 'loyal and peaceable subjects,' " they " 'would not regret being stopped for a day . . . if otherwise, he was acting according to his duty' " (290).

In Cooper's story the relationship between economic expansion and the power of the state is even more apparent, for there is a clear connection between the seizure of the land from the Indians and the upholding of this seizure in the name of the law. Cooper speaks of the Indians as a "wronged and humbled people" (213), and elsewhere in *The Prairie* their victimization is discussed in more specific terms. Mahtoree asserts that the whites would leave the Indians in a state of perpetual weakness. " 'The Big-knives are very wise, and they are men: all of them would be warriors. They would leave the Redskins to dig roots and hoe the corn' " (243). Natty, who himself resents " 'the waste and wickedness of the settlements' " (433), is no less outspoken on the subject of white injustice. He calls the Indians " 'the rightful owners of the country' " (23), and when asked by Hard-Heart, " 'Is a nation to be sold like the skin of a beaver?' " (215), he replies:

> "But might is right, according to the fashions of the 'arth; and what the strong choose to do, the weak must call justice. If the law of the Wacondah was as much hearkened to, Pawnee, as the laws of the Long-knives, your right to the prairies would be as good as that of the greatest chief in the settlements to the house which covers his head." (216)

The exploitive qualities in the society from which Rob and Natty flee present, however, only a negative explanation for the way of life they choose. That life is given positive shape by the feelings both men have about money, honor, and space.[15] In Rob's case his attitude toward money, although it makes him an outlaw, also makes him sensitive to human needs in a way that is different from someone with a conventional concern for profit and loss. Nicol Jarvie describes how in his business dealings Rob gave back money " 'if he thought his chapman had made a hard bargain' " or " 'if he thought the buyer was a puir man, and couldna stand the loss' " (246). The Bailie's remarks point to the fact that, when it comes to a question of business credit or personal honor, Rob always affirms the importance of the latter. Indeed, the Bailie's own departure from Rob illustrates the dramatic nature of this choice. While the Bailie offers to help Rob out of financial difficulties, Rob offers a passionate defense of his cousin's honor:

> After kissing each other very lovingly, and when they were just in the act of parting, the Bailie, in the fulness of his heart, and with a faltering voice, assured his kinsman, "that if ever an hundred pound or even twa hundred, would put him or his family in a settled way, he need but just send his line to the Saut-Market;" and Rob, grasping his basket hilt with one hand, and shaking Mr. Jarvie's heartily with the other, protested, "that if ever any body should affront his kinsman, and he would but let him ken, he would stow the lugs out of his head, were he the best man in Glasgow." (361)

In Natty's case his attitude toward money is no less instrumental in
determining his life. He draws the distinction between his and society's beliefs when he observes, with a combination of deference and
irony, " 'I know that when a poor man talks of credit he deals in a
delicate word, according to the fashions of the world' " (438). But
it is the way in which Natty has lived his life that makes his remark
carry weight. For it is apparent in *The Prairie* that not only has the
elder Natty spurned wealth—" 'At my time of life, food and clothing
be all that is needed' " (17)—but the younger Natty has based his
life on a rejection of financial as well as social respectability, " 'I
might have been a congress-man, or perhaps a governor, years
agone . . . and there are them still living in the Otsego mountains,
as I hope, who would gladly have given me a palace for my dwelling.
But what are riches without content?' " (434).

For Rob and Natty, however, freedom from the usual concern
with money has its most complete expression in pastoral rather than
in humanistic terms. It is in nature and, most specifically, in their
sense of the harmony between man and not-man that Rob and Natty
find the most intense meaning.[16] Rob could never, in the fashion of
Nicol Jarvie, look at a highland lake and imagine a plan for draining
it in such a way as "to preserve a portion of the lake just deep
enough and broad enough for the purposes of water-carriage, so
that coal-barges and gabbards should pass as easily between Dum-
barton and Glenfalloch as between Glasgow and Greenock" (362).
Likewise it would be impossible for Natty to use the woods in the
manner that he sees the settlers doing: " 'They scourge the very
'arth with their axes. Such hills and hunting grounds as I have seen
stripped of the gifts of the Lord, without remorse or shame!' " (80).
As far as Rob and Natty are concerned, the wilderness must be seen
with an awe that reflects man's dependence on a beauty and time-
lessness beyond his control. Rob is aware that he and his clan are
" 'living as our fathers did a thousand years since' " (353), but he
also knows that they draw their strength from such a life. When
Frank Osbaldistone offers Rob military employment, Rob is sure it
would be fatal:

"But the heather that I have trode upon when living, must bloom over me when I am dead—my heart would sink, and my arm would shrink and wither like fern in the frost, were I to lose sight of my native hills; nor has the world a scene that would console me for the loss of rocks and cairns, wild as they are, that you see around us." (354)

Natty's desire to end his life in the wilderness virtually duplicates Rob's. He refuses Captain Middleton's offer of support, " 'Let me sleep where I have lived—beyond the din of settlements!' " (450), and reaffirms what he told Mahtoree earlier in *The Prairie:*

"I passed the spring, summer, and autumn of life among the trees. The winter of my days had come, and found me where I loved to be, in the quiet—ay, and in the honesty of the woods! . . . the axes of the choppers awoke me. . . . but I had heard of these vast and naked fields, and I came hither to escape the wasteful temper of my people." (246)

That Rob and Natty are willing to continue a way of life that is doomed does not, however, blind them to the needs of others or to the reality of their situation. Rob sees the troubles that await his sons and is " 'vexed' " with the idea of " 'Hamish and Robert living their father's life' " (350). Natty advises Paul Hover, a younger and more genteel version of himself, that he and his wife would be happier if they left the prairies and accepted " 'the ways of the inner country' " (438).[17] The significance of Rob's and Natty's consistency is that it leaves them uncompromised, and in so doing, dramatizes the worth and the passion of their heroism.

III   Indeed, even when the two books shift to more critical judgments of Rob and Natty, those judgments reflect the tragedy implicit in Francis Parkman's observation, "Civilization has a destroying as well as a creating power. . . . [and must] sweep from before it a class of men, its own precursors and pioneers, so remarkable in their virtues and faults that few will see their extinction without regret."[18] Scott and Cooper never suggest that the defects in Rob's and Natty's vision are a result of defects in their moral integrity or courage. In each book the problem with the latter's way of life is that it cannot cope with certain kinds of complexity.

The cultural shortcomings of Rob's and Natty's vision are reflected by their lack of interest in what, to Scott and Cooper, were "refined" forms of conduct. In both novels an equation is made between apartness from society and apartness from culture. Frank Osbaldistone draws this distinction as he leaves London for the North:

> As the hum of London died away on my ear, the distant peal of her steeples more than once sounded to my ears the admonitory, "Turn again," erst heard by her future Lord Mayor; and when I looked back from Highgate on her dusky magnificence, I felt as if I were leaving behind me comfort, opulence, the charms of society, and all the pleasures of cultivated life. (23)

Cooper makes a similar observation and adds to it a theory on the growth of nations:

> The gradations of society, from that state which is called refined to that which approaches as near barbarity as connection with an intelligent people will readily allow, are to be traced from the bosom of the States, where wealth, luxury, and the arts are beginning to seat themselves, to those distant and ever-receding borders which mark the skirts and announce the approach of the nation. . . . (69)

This same logic is later applied to Rob and Natty, whose intellectual and cultural shortcomings are seen as a product of their isolation. At their first meeting Frank observes how Rob has been stunted by the life he has led:

> I was tempted from curiosity to dispute the ground with him myself, confiding in my knowledge of the world, extended as it was by my residence abroad, and in the stores with which a tolerable education had possessed my mind. In the latter respect, he offered no competition, and it was easy to see that his natural powers had never been cultivated by education. (35)

The description of Natty, given by the grandfather of Captain Middleton and repeated by Middleton, is almost identical in its emphasis:

"The man I speak of was of great simplicity of mind but of sterling worth. . . . In short, he was a noble shoot from the stock of human nature, which never could attain its proper elevation and importance, for no other reason than it grew in the forest. . . ." (128)

Even more serious are the political difficulties that arise out of Rob's and Natty's vision. For by virtue of their belief in personal freedom and their opposition to the way the law functions, Rob and Natty are in conflict with a political system in which, to quote Burke, "each person has at once divested himself of the first fundamental right of uncovenanted man, that is to judge for himself and to assert his own cause."[19] Scott notes this problem in his introduction when he observes:

> It is this strong contrast betwixt the civilized and cultivated mode of life on the one side of the Highland line, and the wild and lawless adventures which were habitually undertaken and achieved by one who dwelt on the opposite side of that ideal boundary, which creates the interest attached to his [Rob Roy's] name. (xxi)

Cooper discusses the same situation at the start of his novel:

> The resemblance between the American borderer and his European prototype is singular, though not always uniform. Both might be called without restraint, the one being above, the other beyond the reach of the law—brave, because they were inured to danger—proud, because they were independent—and vindictive, because each was the avenger of his own wrongs. (69)

In Rob's and Natty's hands the political rights Burke says man must yield to the state portend only limited dangers for society. Despite his temper, Rob is not given to cruelty or to rashness. As he tells Frank Osbaldistone, " 'Here I stand, have been in twenty frays, and never hurt man but when I was in het bluid . . .' " (353). Natty, an older man than Rob, is even more restrained. He insists that " 'blood is not to be spilt, to save the life of one so useless, and so near his time' " (25), and in defense of his own past maintains that " 'though my hand has been needed in putting down wickedness and oppression, it has never struck a blow of which its owner will be ashamed to hear' " (410). But the self-control Rob and Natty exercise is not maintained by others. In both books the kind of freedom they decline to abuse is severely abused by others and allows redress of the most elementary wrongdoing to lapse into vengeance. In *Rob Roy* the traitor Morris, who has helped the British capture Rob, is drowned on orders from Helen MacGregor:

> The victim was held fast by some, while others, binding a large heavy stone in a plaid, tied it round his neck, and others again eagerly stripped him of some part of his dress. Half-naked, and thus manacled, they hurled him into the lake, there about twelve feet deep, with a loud halloo of vindictive triumph,—above which, however, his last death-shriek, the yell of mortal agony, was distinctly heard. (311)

In *The Prairie* Abiram White is hanged by Ishmael Bush for shooting one of Bush's sons:

> But all was now in the stillness of death. The grim and convulsed countenance of the victim was at times brought full into the light of the moon, and again as the wind lulled, the fatal rope drew a dark line across its bright disk. The squatter raised his rifle with extreme care, and fired. The cord was cut and the body came lumbering to earth, a heavy and insensible mass. (426)

The tone of these scenes, in which the first executioner is the wife and the second, the father of the wronged party, makes their implications all the more dramatic. In *Rob Roy* Frank Osbaldistone and Nicol Jarvie are more affected by this "single deed of violence and cruelty" than a day of battle in which they have seen killing on an "extended scale" (312), and Rob, who admits that his wife has " 'deep wrongs to avenge,' " still asserts that " 'such a deed might make one forswear kin, clan, county, wife, and bairns' " (338). In *The Prairie* the killing of Abiram White is both less brutal and more justified but still not free from revenge. In order to act as judge and jury Ishmael must finally assume the role of an Old Testament God and declare, " 'I have but little knowledge of the ways of the courts, though there is a rule that is known unto all, and which teaches that an 'eye must be returned for an eye,' and 'a tooth for a tooth' " (400–401).

One need not concentrate on extreme examples, however, in

order to point out the dangers inherent in Rob's and Natty's vision. The social limitations of their vision (specifically, the difficulty of extending it on a broad scale) are revealed in the daily life that Sir Hildebrand Osbaldistone and Ishmael Bush lead. In their wish to remain unfettered and in their skepticism of authority, Sir Hildebrand and Ishmael are the doubles of Rob and Natty. Sir Hildebrand is a Catholic, a Jacobite opposed to the Hanoverian Succession, and a foe of life based on commerce. Ishmael resents the stratification of society, questions the justice of property rights, and refuses to deal with courts of law. Yet when these qualities, which are virtues in Rob and Natty, are combined in Sir Hildebrand and Ishmael, they turn out to be not only grotesque but socially destructive. For Sir Hildebrand, all that freedom means is more time for fox hunting and drinking. A Scottish version of Fielding's Squire Western, Sir Hildebrand is a man with few redeeming qualities. Although kind to his niece, who he expects will marry one of his sons, he is indifferent to nearly everyone and everything else. His estate is "reduced to almost nothing by his own carelessness and the debauchery of his sons and household" (371), and in the end he too is reduced to almost nothing. As Frank observes, Sir Hildebrand "rather ceased to exist than died of any positive struggle" (373).

Ishmael Bush's primary virtue is that, like Sir Hildebrand, he is kind to a niece who he expects will marry one of his sons. In every other matter Ishmael combines the worst qualities of a man leading a border life. As Henry Nash Smith notes, Ishmael is "made to commit crime, not only against nature, but also against civilization."[20] He and his family strip a "small but suitable spot of its burden of forest, as effectually, and almost as promptly, as if a whirlwind had passed along the place" (13), and he personally helps in the kidnapping of Inez de Certavallos, whom he admires only for the ransom she will bring. In the end all that Cooper can do with Ishmael and his family is have them fade out of sight and continue with their "lawless and semi-barbarous" (427) existence.

Scott's and Cooper's scrutiny of, or more accurately, de-romanticizing of the implications of Rob's and Natty's vision represents more than just criticism by them. It is a way of justifying the importance of their conventional heroes, Frank Osbaldistone and Captain

Middleton, whose view of the future is the one that in fact prevails in both stories.

IV   In virtually all that they do, Frank and Captain Middleton reflect the kind of practical intelligence and controlled decency one expects of conventional heroes.[21] Yet their ordinariness is not the result of banality, but historical circumstances in which, to quote David Daiches, "man's destiny, at least in the modern world, is to find his testing time not amid the sound of trumpets but in the daily struggles and recurring crises of personal and social life."[22] Within the context of *Rob Roy* and *The Prairie* the world Frank and Middleton stand for reflects the ability of society at its best to unite disparate people, create order, and come to terms with the past.

For Scott and Cooper, the uniting of two cultures, each with its own traditions and character, had enormous appeal. They did not regard the drawbacks of such a venture as equal to its advantages. Scott traces the hostility between the English and the Scottish to "the natural consequences of their existence as separate and rival states" (34), and Cooper speaks of "some little time" being necessary to "blend the discrepant elements" of a society composed of Americans and those once ruled by the Spanish (178). But in both books national antagonisms are seen as basically irrational. Frank describes his youthful "aversion to the Northern inhabitants of Britain" as one of his inherited "prejudices" (34), and Cooper uses the term "barriers of prejudice" (178) when speaking of the rivalry between Americans and other citizens of the Louisiana Territory. Thus in each story union between people living so near one another is made to seem not only possible but extremely beneficial.

The benefits of such a union are revealed by Frank and Middleton, who, unlike Rob and Natty, have needs that cannot be fulfilled in isolation. In *Rob Roy* the economic advantages of national union are shown by the help Nicol Jarvie gives the firm of Osbaldistone and Tresham. It is he who discloses how dangerous the anti-Scottish prejudices of Frank's father can be, and it is his willingness to be agent for the Scottish business of Osbaldistone and Tresham that assures the firm prosperity and stability in Scotland. In *The Prairie* Don Augustin de Certavallos proves almost as much help to Middleton by placing him in a position where his talents can be noticed. Although Middleton's success reflects his abilities, it is, as Cooper notes, the "local importance Middleton had acquired, by his union with so affluent a proprietor as Don Augustin, united to his personal merit, [that] attracted the attention of the government" (441).

The marriages of Frank and Middleton are equally important in emphasizing what the union of disparate people can mean. Their marriages succeed only because deep religious prejudices are overcome. Frank is at first bitterly opposed by Die Vernon's father. "Sir Frederick Vernon was a rigid Catholic, who thought the path of salvation too narrow to be trodden by an heretic" (389). Middleton must counter the objections of Inez and her father. "Religion formed a stubborn and nearly irremovable obstacle with both" (180). Yet Frank and Middleton prove that personal feelings, if grounded in a respect for traditional differences, can provide a sounder basis for happiness than unquestioning adherence to custom. Frank's marriage to the pro-Scottish, Catholic Die Vernon parallels the Act of Union between England and Scotland in 1707, and Middleton's marriage to Inez de Certavallos, who is Catholic and of Spanish descent, corresponds to the acquisition of the Louisiana Territory by America in 1803.

Frank and Middleton also demonstrate that, although modern society creates problems peculiar to its largeness, when operating properly, it brings into play forces for correcting these problems and establishing order. Because they represent powerful institutions, Frank and Middleton are in a position to cope with difficulties before which Rob and Natty can only retreat. As a member of a trading firm, Frank, in conjunction with his father, is able to combat the people who take advantage of his family's credit (in a parallel situation Rob finds that he must become an outlaw). As a soldier and a legislator, Middleton is among those with authority to say how the new territories will be run (Natty, on the other hand, must continually move west in order to avoid conflict). The significance of these accomplishments is further emphasized by generalizations that are made in both books. In speaking of international commerce, Frank asserts, " 'It connects nation with nation, relieves the wants, and contributes to the wealth of all; and is to the general commonwealth of the civilized world what the daily intercourse of ordinary life is to private society, or rather, what air and food are to our bodies' " (12). In discussing the impact of the Louisiana Purchase on those living in that territory, Cooper observes how "the transfer raised them from the condition of subjects to the more enviable distinction of citizens in a government of laws. The new rulers exercised their functions with discretion, and wielded their delegated authority without offense" (178).

The significance of the political union and social order Frank and Middleton support would be lost, however, if it were not tied to the respect they have for the past. In both novels it is clear that the forces of progress can be kept within bounds only when it is under-stood that change disrupts an older and meaningful way of life. This feeling for the past does not require Frank and Middleton to alter the basic course of their lives. Frank's sympathy for Rob does not stop him from offering to fight on the side of the government during the rebellion of 1715, and Middleton's awareness of the injustices committed against the Indians does not cause him to resign his army commission. But Frank and Middleton are changed because of their involvement in the world Rob and Natty represent. They are freed from the unfeelingness of those who are loyal only to the modern world. Frank may accept the virtues of commerce, but unlike his father's clerk, he can never speak of the Golden Rule in mercantile language, " 'Let A do to B, as he would have B do to him; the product will give the rule of conduct required' " (11). Similarly, although Middleton is willing to assert the authority of the govern-ment over land to which the Indians have a birthright, he can never be included in Mahtoree's statement, " 'Your warriors think the master of life has made the whole earth white' " (224).

These differences in the conduct of Frank and Middleton often appear as matters of style, but there is a substance to the style. Frank and Middleton are finally allied not only with those responsible for bringing about change but with those who believe in the past. Un-like his father, Frank is able to occupy his family's Northumberland home and feel an attachment to the Highlands that does not betray his position as a merchant. Middleton, through his friendship with Natty, is able to establish contact with someone who fought beside his grandfather and knew the Indian in whose honor he was given the middle name of Uncas. The result is that only Rob and Natty, who wish to turn their backs on the present, have a greater feeling for the past than Frank and Middleton. The latter, on the other hand, accept the more difficult task of treating the past as a link to the present. It is a commitment that in its compromises and complexities lacks an obvious splendor. Yet it is the one commitment in *Rob Roy* and *The Prairie* that acknowledges the inevitability of societal growth and the need for society to take into account the wilderness life it threatens to destroy.

V   In neither novel is a serious historical alternative offered in place of the course of action Frank and Middleton follow. Where the two stories differ is in the emphasis they put on the defeat of the way of life Rob and Natty represent. In Cooper's novel Natty's death, " 'When I am gone there will be an end of my race' " (450), is far more serious than the obscurity into which Rob fades: "he died in old age and by a peaceful death, some time around the year 1733" (399). This difference in emphasis, which is of decisive importance at the end of each book, is consistent with earlier treatment of Rob and Natty. Although both are folk heroes, the implications of their heroism vary in each novel. Rob is an historical figure reduced to human proportions; his escapes are daring, his bravery is extraordinary. But within the context of Scott's novel these qualities are not nearly so revealing as others. As Georg Lukacs has written, "Scott's great art consists precisely in individualizing his historical heroes in such a way that certain, purely individual traits of character, quite peculiar to them, are brought into a very complex, very live relationship with the age in which they live."[23] Natty, on the other hand, may reflect the Daniel Boone legend, but he is not a surrogate for Daniel Boone. Although frequently described in mundane detail, he is finally larger than life. A. N. Kaul is not exaggerating when he writes, "The fictional career of Natty Bumppo is perhaps the clearest statement in literature of the archetypal American experience. . . . it seems almost as simple-minded in its moral idealism as Bradford's history of America. Yet perhaps it is the simplicity that helps to give it the distinctive outline of a memorable and meaningful myth."[24]

These differences are implicit in the first scenes in which Rob and Natty appear. Rob is described with the detail we find in a Dutch genre painting.[25] His clothes, his speech, the inn where he is staying are reproduced with an exactness that leaves little to the imagination. The impression one gets is of a man who possesses considerable ordinariness as well as great strength:

> He had the hard features and athletic form, said to be peculiar to his country, together with the natural intonation and slow pedantic mode of expression, arising from a desire to avoid peculiarities of idiom or dialect. . . . His dress was as coarse as it could be, being still decent; and, at a time when great expense was lavished upon wardrobe . . . this indicated mediocrity of circumstances, if not poverty. (34)

By contrast, the initial portrait of Natty reflects Cooper's admiration for the Hudson River School of painting.[26] Natty is posed against a sweeping view of the landscape; his presence is heightened by the dramatic use of lighting, and the result is suggestive of his closeness to a world moved by powerful forces:

> The sun had fallen below the crest of the nearest wave of the prairie, leaving the usual rich and glowing train on its track. In the center of this flood of fiery light, a human form appeared. . . . The figure was colossal; the attitude musing and melancholy; and the situation directly in the route of the travellers. (8)

Scott was, of course, capable of writing an equally spectacular scene for the purpose of introducing Rob, but that he chose not to makes perfect sense. Such a beginning would contradict the fact that in *Rob Roy* it is Frank Osbaldistone who is the most important character and sole narrator. Indeed, Scott's story follows a classic pattern in which, as William R. Taylor has noted, "the central figure sets out from society, has his adventure, and returns to the everyday world at the end."[27] *The Prairie* does not, on the other hand, fit this formula. The most dramatically important figure in the story is

Natty, who, in a novel deeply concerned with society, remains outside society. Moreover, Cooper in the role of omniscient author makes sure that his hero is never eclipsed by any other character.

The significance of these differences reaches fruition in the endings of the two books. In Scott's novel the stress is ultimately on Frank's success: his marriage, his return to his father's good graces, and his assumption of a partnership in the firm of Osbaldistone and Tresham. At this point Rob is of little concern. Frank resumes the conversational tone with which the book began, and one is reminded that the story is really a letter from him to his business partner: "I have no more of romantic adventure to tell, nor, indeed, anything to communicate farther, since the latter incidents of my life are so well known to one who has shared, with the most friendly sympathy, the joys as well as the sorrows by which its scenes have been chequered" (399). In contrast to the aged Frank's epistolary style, the writing at the end of Cooper's novel has a pastoral intensity about it. Middleton's marriage, his prosperity, his fame as a legislator are summarized rather than lingered over. All attention is focused on the timeless world that Natty represents. His dying, like his living, is in harmony with the forces of nature and the cosmos: "When opened, his gaze seemed fastened on the clouds which hung around the western horizon, reflecting the bright colors, and giving form and loveliness to the tints of an American sunset. The hour—the calm beauty of the season—the occasion, all conspired to fill the spectators with solemn awe" (452).

Natty's magnificence, "the air of grandeur and humility which were so remarkable united in the mien of the trapper" (452), does not, to reemphasize a point made earlier, lessen the need for the kind of society Frank and Middleton believe in. But it does mean that for Cooper, in contrast to Scott, this development is to be judged from a perspective in which the vision the new society rules out rather than the progress it makes possible is most important. And it does explain why, for all their historic and poetic similarities, the Waverly Novels and Leatherstocking Tales should seem to face in opposite directions: in the one case, forward; in the other, backward.

NOTES

1. Despite his dislike of being called the "American Scott," Cooper often compared his work and Scott's. To a friend like the inventor Samuel F. B. Morse, he had no qualms in writing, *"The Heidenmauer* is not equal to *The Bravo,* but it is a good book and better than two-thirds of Scott's." (Quoted in *The Letters and Journals of James Fenimore Cooper,* ed. James Franklin Beard, vol. 2 [Cambridge, Mass., 1960], p. 310.)

2. Ibid., pp. 83–4.

3. Thomas Lounsbury, *James Fenimore Cooper* (Boston, 1882), p. 59.

4. A modern example of the kind of criticism Lounsbury has in mind is reflected in F. R. Leavis's observation, "Scott was a kind of inspired folklorist qualified to have done in fiction something analogous to the ballad opera. . . . Out of Scott a bad tradition came. It spoiled Fenimore Cooper, who had new and first-hand interests and the makings of a distinguished novelist. (*The Great Tradition* [New York, 1963], pp. 5–6.) See also Anthony Burgess, "Said Mr. Cooper to His Wife: 'You Know, I Could Write Something Better Than That,' " *New York Times Magazine* (May 7, 1972), 108, 112–14, 115.

5. David Levin, *History as Romantic Art* (New York, 1959), p. 15.

6. Donald Davie, *The Heyday of Sir Walter Scott* (London, 1961), pp. 101–147; George Dekkar, *James Fenimore Cooper the Novelist* (London, 1967), pp. 20–42.

7. Mark Twain, *Life on the Mississippi* (New York, 1911), pp. 375–8 and "Fenimore Cooper's Literary Offenses," *The Shock of Recognition,* ed. Edmund Wilson (New York, 1955), pp. 582–94.

8. Leslie Fiedler, *Love and Death in the American Novel* (New York, 1967), p. 165.

9. Ibid.

10. All page references are to the following paperback edition: Sir Walter Scott, *Rob Roy* (Boston: Houghton Mifflin, 1956).

11. All page references are to the following paperback edition: James Fenimore Cooper, *The Prairie* (New York: Holt, Rinehart, and Winston, 1950).

12. See Georg Lukacs, *The Historical Novel* (Boston, 1963), pp. 63–5.

13. This subject is explored in Francis Hart, *Scott's Novels: The Plotting of Historical Survival* (Charlottesville, 1966), p. 32.

14. George Macaulay Trevelyan, *England Under Queen Anne: The Peace and the Protestant Succession* (London, 1934), p. 233.

15. The best discussion of spatial vision is to be found in R. W. B. Lewis, *The American Adam* (Chicago, 1955), pp. 98–100.

16. This approach to landscape is treated in Leo Marx, *The Machine in the Garden* (New York, 1964), p. 23.

17. The relationship of Paul Hover to Natty is discussed in Henry Nash Smith, *The Virgin Land* (New York, 1961), pp. 74–6.

18. "The Works of Fenimore Cooper," *Francis Parkman: Representative Selections*, ed. Wilbur Schramm (New York, 1938), p. 207.

19. Edmund Burke, *Works*, vol. 2 (London, 1867), p. 332.

20. Henry Nash Smith, "Introduction," *The Prairie* (New York, 1955), p. xvii.

21. George Lukacs, *The Historical Novel*, p. 33.

22. David Daiches, "Scott's Achievement as a Novelist," *Literary Essays* (London, 1956), p. 88.

23. George Lukacs, *The Historical Novel*, p. 47.

24. A. N. Kaul, *The American Vision* (New Haven, 1964), p. 120.

25. The most complete discussion of Scott and Dutch genre painting is in Mario Praz, *The Hero in Eclipse* (London, 1956), pp. 54–64.

26. A helpful discussion of Cooper and the Hudson River School of painting is in Howard Mumford Jones, "Prose and Pictures: James Fenimore Cooper," *Tulane Studies in English*, vol. 3 (New Orleans, 1952), pp. 133–54.

27. William R. Taylor, *Cavalier and Yankee* (Garden City, 1963), p. 84.

4

Nathaniel Hawthorne and George Eliot

I   In an introductory essay to *Adam Bede*, F. R. Leavis writes:

> George Eliot had read *The Scarlet Letter* when it came out, and (what doesn't surprise us) expressed great admiration for Hawthorne. The idea that Hawthorne's influence can be discovered in *Adam Bede* was prompted, as it came to me, by the name of Hetty. Once one thinks of Hester Prynne, the effect of the suggestion has its compelling significance, even if one is at first inclined to dismiss the echo as mere chance. The treatment of the agonized conscience in Arthur Donnithorne convinces one before long that in the treatment of the seduction theme *The Scarlet Letter* has told significantly. This real affinity (for all the differences of temperament and art between the two authors) brings home to one, in fact, that the association of names was more than a chance clue. One notes, further, that Hawthorne's male sinner is also Arthur, Arthur Dimmesdale for George Eliot's Arthur Donnithorne.[1]

The aim of Leavis's comparison is to show, "We have here, unmistakably, a case of that profound kind of influence of which the artist in whom it works is unaware."[2] But as telling as it is, Leavis's analysis is suggestive rather than thorough. The relationship between *The Scarlet Letter* and *Adam Bede* that is most important centers on the way Hawthorne's and Eliot's "treatment of the seduction theme" leads to their reexamination of the Biblical dilemma of the fall.

The nature of this relationship comes directly into focus when we compare *The Scarlet Letter* and *Adam Bede* with *Madame Bovary*.[3] Indeed, the difference between Hawthorne's and Eliot's intentions and Flaubert's is even apparent in their choice of titles. It is Emma, with her dreams and her sexual energies, who is the subject of Flaubert's story, and it is her struggle to realize these desires that forms the basis of his novel. Flaubert's criticism of French life—of the Church, of the aristocracy, of the provinces—is intense, but the most dramatic parts of his novel center on Emma's love affairs. Once she finds herself trapped and unable to begin again, her suicide is as natural as it is horrible. By contrast, Hawthorne's and Eliot's novels achieve momentum after the sexual infidelity of their heroines is brought into the open. It is the way in which the sexual conduct of Hester and Hetty is understood, not the way in which it is carried out, that is the essence of *The Scarlet Letter* and *Adam Bede*. There is minimal erotic or clinical description in either book, not because Hester, Hetty, and the two Arthurs are less sensual than Emma and her lovers, but because the meaning of their lives depends on consequences that go far beyond their love affairs. Unlike Flaubert's novel, in which suffering produces little change in Emma's romanticism or Charles's dullness or Rodolphe's vanity, in Hawthorne's and Eliot's novels the meaning of the two love affairs must be measured in terms of widely varying alterations in consciousness.

The narrative technique of the three books emphasizes this difference. In contrast to Hawthorne and Eliot, who respond to the increasing complexity of their novels by addressing the reader, making comments on characters, and revealing ambiguities of their own, Flaubert remains at a distance in his story, and his attitude toward his characters must be inferred, as Harry Levin has pointed out, "from his almost cinematographic manipulation of detail" rather than from any direct commentary.[4] The result is that as *Madame Bovary* moves from intrigue to intrigue, it is not new insight into Emma's problems that Flaubert conveys so much as a fuller realization of ironies that have always been present in her situation. On the other hand, in *The Scarlet Letter* and *Adam Bede* Hawthorne and Eliot prepare the way for far-reaching changes in perspective. The original tensions between society and Hester and Hetty are no longer the principal concerns at the end of the two stories. These tensions have become subordinate to the broader and ultimately religious set of problems that develops as the emphasis of both books shifts from the societal response to Hester and Hetty to the response of those whose lives are directly affected by each woman.

II   The description of society in *The Scarlet Letter* and *Adam Bede* is in many respects a traditional one that concerns itself with matters of class and status. In Boston "ruffs, painfully wrought bands, and gorgeously embroidered gloves" are "readily allowed to individuals dignified by rank or wealth," although "sumptuary laws forbade these and similar extravagances to the plebian order" (82).[5] In Hayslope the aristocratic Miss Lydia Irwine, "adjusting her own lace," can give away a "grogram gown and a piece of flannel" to the winner of the sack race, and then comment, " 'I should not think of encouraging a love of finery in young women of that class' " (233).[6] But class tensions and the struggle for status are finally secondary factors in both books. To be sure, status makes it all the more difficult for Dimmesdale, who is at "the head of the social system" (199) to acknowledge his involvement with Hester, and status also draws Hetty to Arthur Donnithorne, while making marriage out of the question for her and the young squire. Yet Hawthorne and Eliot pay relatively little attention to these kinds of questions. The importance of society in *The Scarlet Letter* and *Adam Bede* is that it has a restrictiveness that so distorts human relationships and human error that it paves the way for the tragedies that follow from Hester's and Hetty's actions. In both novels the narrative is punctuated by chapters explicitly devoted to social analysis: for example, "The Market Place," "The Governor's Hall," "New England Holiday" in *The Scarlet Letter;* "The Workshop," "Church," "The Games" in *Adam Bede.* But whether we focus on these chapters or on the broader web of social relations in each book, the consequences are the same. First, society forces Hester's and Hetty's private lives into the open (it brings Hester to trial and causes such shame in Hetty that she abandons her child); then it so cruelly passes judgment on both women that neither they nor anyone close to them is ever the same.

In each novel the shortcomings of the popular judgment of Hester and Hetty are first revealed in the failure of society to be aware of its own limitations. The style in which the people of Boston and Hayslope are described has many parallels with Dutch genre painting (an art form Hawthorne and Eliot both admired).[7] The observation is highly detailed, and in its exploration of dress, buildings, and facial expressions creates a strong picture of daily life. Yet it is in their departure from the flattering nature of genre painting that the marrow of Hawthorne's and Eliot's art lies. For what both books reveal is that the people of Boston and Hayslope are blindly at war with the natural and the spontaneous. Hawthorne speaks of the "grim rigidity that petrified the bearded physiognomies" (51) of the Puritans, and then goes on to describe them as:

> a community, which owed its origin and progress, and its present state of development, not to the impulses of youth, but to the stern and tempered energies of manhood, and the sombre sagacity of age; accomplishing so much, precisely because it imagined and hoped so little. . . . out of the whole human family, it would not have been easy to select the same number of wise and virtuous persons, who should be less capable of sitting in judgment on an erring woman's heart, and disentangling its mesh of good and evil, than the sages of rigid aspect towards whom Hester Prynne now turned her face. (65)

Hawthorne's description of the Puritans' inability to judge questions of passion or guilt has its parallel in two scenes in *Adam Bede*. In the first of these scenes George Eliot describes the effect of Dinah Morris's sermon on a typical listener:

> Now and then there was a new arrival; perhaps a slouching labourer, who, having eaten his supper, came out to look at the unusual scene with a slow bovine gaze, willing to hear what any one had to say in explanation of it, but by no means excited enough to ask a question. (17)

In the second scene the pregnant Hetty realizes she cannot expect help from family or neighbors: "people who were somewhat hard in their feelings even towards poverty, who lived among the fields, and had little pity for want and rags . . . but held them as a mark of idleness and vice" (317).

What makes this unfeelingness on the part of the people of Boston and Hayslope so dangerous, however, is that it is justified, even furthered, by their religious life. Hawthorne is not being ironic when he observes that for the Puritans "forms of authority were felt to possess the sacredness of divine institutions" (65),[8] and despite the kindness of a minister like Mr. Irwine, Hetty is not mistaken in believing that for someone in difficulty "the 'parish' was next to the prison in obloquy" (317). In both communities the church, which is supported by public taxes, consists of people whose feelings are alien to any Pauline concept of charity. The residents of Boston are "a people amongst whom religion and law were almost identical" and "in whose character both were so thoroughly interfused, that the mildest and severest acts of public discipline were alike made venerable and awful" (52). The Puritans adopt an attitude toward Hester exactly opposite the one Jesus followed when the woman taken in adultery was brought before him and he challenged those who were without sin to cast the first stone. In *Adam Bede* religion, law, and custom serve the same ends with only slightly less oppressiveness. A woman "found against the church wall . . . nearly dead with cold and hunger" (317) is treated as an object of shame, and the maid who leaves dirt in the corner is told that " 'anybody 'ud think you'd never been brought up among Christians' " (65).[9] For people in Hayslope and the surrounding towns, religion is above all a way of controlling behavior and events. In church faith rests on the ability of the service "to ward off harm and bring blessing" (168); in court the "chaplain in his canonicals" is appropriately seated "behind" the judge (365).

Thus it is logical that the Puritans should regard it as a sign of " 'their great mercy and tenderness of heart' " to place Hester on the pillory and require her to wear the scarlet letter for " 'the rest of her natural life' " (64), and it is appropriate that Hetty, whose trial takes place in nearby Stoniton, should be sentenced with "no recommendation to mercy" (365) in a court of justice, which "through the rest of the year was haunted with the shadowy memories of kings and queens" (360). Indeed, even the extreme reactions to both women are not contradictory of basic community values. The woman in *The Scarlet Letter* who is "the most pitiless" of Hester's "self-constituted judges" (53) reflects the thinking of people who in general have "a moral diet not a whit more refined" than the "beef and ale of their native land" (52). Her spitefulness is based on an appeal to community traditions: "The woman has brought shame upon us all, and ought to die. Is there not law for it? Truly there is, both in the Scripture and the statute book" (53). The same kind of response is true of Martin Poyser, who reacts to Hetty, a member of his family, with a "scorching sense of disgrace, which neutralized all other sensibility" (347). His assertion, " 'I'll not go nigh her, nor ever see her again, by my own will. She's made our bread bitter to us for all our lives to come' " (347) is directly attributable to his being "under the yoke of traditional impressions" (347).

The most typical picture the people of Boston and Hayslope have of Hester and Hetty is clearly one in which the two women are distorted beyond recognition. When Hester visits Governor Bellingham, she discovers that in the mirror formed by his armor the symbol of her crime is her most visible aspect: "the scarlet letter was represented in exaggerated and gigantic proportions, so as to be greatly the most prominent feature of her appearance. In truth, she seemed absolutely hidden behind it" (105). When the usually gentle schoolmaster, Bartle Massey, speaks of Hetty, she is reduced to vermin, " 'I mean it's stuff and nonsense for the innocent to care about her being hanged. For my own part, I think the sooner such women are put out o' the world the better; . . . What good will you do by keeping such vermin alive?' " (350–1). The result is that in *The Scarlet Letter* and *Adam Bede* societal judgment of Hester and Hetty reveals not only its own flaws but the desperate need for alternative responses to both women.[10]

III   This need is not, however, readily filled. When Hawthorne's and Eliot's emphases shift to the characters who make up the sexual triangles in their books, the responses of each of these figures that provide the most obvious basis of comparison and contrast with society reveal only subtler limitations in understanding. The clearest case in point is that of Roger Chillingworth and the early Adam Bede, who admits " 'there's more pride nor love in my soul' " (172). Both of these men are guided by impulses not unlike those of the townspeople of Boston and Hayslope. They see themselves as the victims of wrongdoing, and they appropriate the right to punish the persons who have hurt them. Accordingly, the questions they raise are extensions of questions raised by the failure of society to come to terms with Hester and Hetty: Who is so innocent that he has a right to punish? Who is so knowing that he can judge the motives of another man? As it turns out, neither Chillingworth nor Adam can act as avenger without destroying himself, and the men whom they would punish are sufficiently pained by their own judgment of events.

Chillingworth's and Adam's roles in the downfall of Hester and Hetty are first reflected in the inability of either to gain the heart of the woman. Chillingworth describes his heart as " 'a habitation large enough for many guests, but lonely and chill, and without a household fire' " (75). Adam confesses, " 'I was always too hard' " (172). These are defects that neither man can put aside merely because he is in love. Chillingworth admits, " 'Mine was the first wrong, when I betrayed thy budding youth into a false and unnatural relation with my decay' " (75). " 'It was my folly and thy weakness. . . . Misshapen from my birthhour, how could I delude myself with the idea that intellectual gifts might veil physical deformity in a young girl's fantasy!' " (74–5). Adam's failure to stir in Hetty "the emotions that make the sweet intoxication of young love" (86) is certainly not altogether his fault. Yet Adam is guilty of relying upon Martin Poyser's approval of him over Hetty's other suitors, and when he comes to see Hetty, it is often less as a lover than as someone with "a degree of accomplishment totally unknown among the richest farmers of the country-side," a man "who carried such authority with all the people round about" and "knew what to say about things, could tell her uncle how to prop the hovel, and had mended the churn in no time" (84).

Under these circumstances it is clear why Chillingworth and

Adam are in no position to punish Hester and Hetty for their infidelity. Such retaliation is not, however, their primary concern. " 'Between thee and me, the scale hangs fairly balanced,' " Chillingworth tells Hester (75). " 'I don't want to blame her,' " Adam says of Hetty (341). It is the men who they believe have led Hester and Hetty astray that Chillingworth and Adam want to punish. " 'I shall seek this man, as I have sought truth in books; as I have sought gold in alchemy,' " Chillingworth tells Hester (76). " 'I'll make him go and look at her in misery. . . . he shan't escape wi' lies this time— I'll fetch him, I'll drag him myself,' " Adam says of Arthur Donnithorne (344). But it is as self-destructive for Chillingworth and Adam to attempt to revenge themselves on Hester's and Hetty's lovers as on the two women. In Chillingworth's case his tormenting of Dimmesdale brings about his ruin. In the words of F. O. Matthiessen, "The physician's own transformation is handled with strictest accord to the Puritans' belief in how an erring mind could become so divorced from God that it lapsed into a state of diabolical possession."[11] As Chillingworth devotes himself to "adding fuel to those fiery tortures which he analyzed and gloated over" (169), his appearance changes until he presents "striking evidence of man's faculty of transforming himself into a devil, if he will only, for a reasonable space of time, undertake a devil's office" (168–9). Dimmesdale is accurate when he says, " 'There is one worse than even the polluted priest! That old man's revenge has been blacker than my sin. He has violated, in cold blood, the sanctity of the human heart' " (194). Adam never goes to Chillingworth's lengths, but in his "desire to punish" (354), he too is in "danger of being led to the commission of some great wrong" (355). Mr. Irwine is right to warn Adam, " 'An act of vengeance on your part against Arthur would simply be another evil added to those we are suffering under: you could not bear the punishment alone; you would entail the worst sorrows on everyone who loves you' " (355). Adam acknowledges the truth of Mr. Irwine's warning when he tells Arthur Donnithorne at their second meeting, " 'I've been a bit hard t' everybody but *her*. . . . I've no right to be hard towards them as have done wrong and repent' " (392).

There is, moreover, no pain that Chillingworth and Adam can

inflict on the two Arthurs that is not essentially gratuitous. The actions of the latter destroy the vision they have of themselves. Dimmesdale is tortured by his conscience. As he tells Hester, " 'were I an atheist,—a man devoid of conscience,—a wretch with coarse and brutal instincts,—I might have found peace, long ere now' " (189–90). There is nowhere Dimmesdale can turn and find refuge, " 'I must stand up in my pulpit, and meet so many eyes turned upward to my face, as if the light of heaven were beaming from it! . . . and then look inward and discern the black reality' " (190). Arthur Donnithorne also " 'has a heart and a conscience' " (354), and as Mr. Irwine tells Adam, Arthur will feel the effects of Hetty's tragedy " 'all his life' " (354). Of course, Arthur Donnithorne's suffering is not as intense as Arthur Dimmesdale's, but it is still a serious step for him to give up his role as country squire and "the patron of new ploughs and drills" (367). Arthur is justified in reminding Adam of the price he is paying for keeping others from leaving Hayslope:

> "If I were going to stay here and act as landlord . . . if I were careless about what I've done . . . you would have some excuse, Adam, for going away and encouraging others to go. You would have some excuse then for trying to make the evil worse. But when I tell you I'm going away for years—when you know what that means for me, how it cuts off every plan of happiness I've ever formed—it is impossible for a sensible man like you to believe that there is any real ground for the Poysers refusing to remain." (391)

In contrast to Chillingworth and Adam, Hester and Hetty react to the situation in which they find themselves by trying to escape it. Both women believe they are misunderstood, and with good reason. Hawthorne's and Eliot's novels reveal not only the narrowness of society in Boston and Hayslope but the worth of Hester's and Hetty's romantic impulses. In each novel the meeting of the lovers is described in pastoral terms that show great sympathy for Hester and Hetty. In *The Scarlet Letter* Hester's meeting with Dimmesdale revives her:

> Her sex, her youth, and the whole richness of her beauty, came back from what men call the irrevocable past, and clustered themselves, with her

maiden hope, and a happiness before unknown, within the magic circle of this hour. (201)

Even the sky and woods, "the sympathy of Nature," respond to the "bliss" (202) of Hester and Arthur:

> And, as if the gloom of the earth and sky had been but the effluence of these two mortal hearts, it vanished with their sorrow. All at once, as with a sudden smile of heaven, forth burst the sunshine, pouring a very flood into the obscure forest, gladdening each green leaf, transmuting the yellow fallen ones to gold, and gleaming down the gray trunks of the solemn trees. (201)

In *Adam Bede* Hetty's love for Arthur is no less magical in its effects:

> As for Hetty, her feet rested on a cloud, and she was borne along by warm zephyrs; she had forgotten her rose-coloured ribbons; she was no more conscious of her limbs than if her childish soul had passed into a water-lily, resting on a liquid bed, and warmed by the midsummer sunbeams. (112)

As in *The Scarlet Letter*, the lovers and the woods are transformed:

> for a long moment time has vanished. He may be a shepherd in Arcadia for ought he knows, he may be the first youth kissing the first maiden, he may be Eros himself, sipping the lips of Psyche—it is all one. (117–18)

Nonetheless, for all their sympathy with Hester's and Hetty's plight, Hawthorne and Eliot finally treat both women's actions as destructive and incomplete. Of Hester, Hawthrone notes, "Shame, Despair, Solitude! These had been her teachers,—stern and wild ones,—and they had made her strong, but taught her much amiss" (198). Of the much weaker Hetty, Eliot observes that "her waking dreams . . . merged in a sleeping life scarcely more fragmentary and confused" (138). Hester's belief that her love and Dimmesdale's " 'had a consecration of its own' " (194) comes to blind her to other truths, and Hetty is limited even more by her "peculiar form of worship" (128), which consists of admiring herself and remembering Arthur Donnithorne's words.[12] Both women are prepared to ignore the past when it does not suit their purposes. " 'Let us not look back. . . . The past is gone!' " (200) Hester tells Dimmesdale.

"Hetty could have cast all her past life behind her, and never cared to be reminded of it again" (132), Eliot observes.

At issue here is the degree to which both women are willing to lose themselves in escape. At times it seems as if their idea of escape is in reality a death wish. Hester finds that "a fearful doubt strove to possess her soul, whether it were not better to send Pearl at once to heaven, and go herself to such futurity as Eternal Justice should provide" (165). Hetty has a time when she thinks it would be best to "wander out of sight, and drown herself where her body would never be found, and no one should know what had become of her" (321). More commonly, however, Hester and Hetty nourish the belief they will be happy if they can just escape the society that has so cruelly judged them.[13] It is with this hope in mind that Hester says to Dimmesdale, " 'Doth the universe lie within the compass of yonder town . . . ? Whither leads yonder forest-track? . . . There thou art free! So brief a journey would bring thee from a world where thou hast been most wretched, to one where thou mayest still be happy!' " (195–6). It is with a similar feeling that Hetty decides, "She must run away; she must hide herself where no familiar eyes could detect her; and *then* the terror of wandering out into the world, of which she knew nothing, made the possibility of going to Arthur a thought which brought some comfort with it" (307).

The result is that the major problems in *The Scarlet Letter* and *Adam Bede* are ones Hester and Hetty seek to evade. Hester would have Dimmesdale take comfort in actions that conceal his guilt, " 'Your present life is not less holy, in very truth, than it seems in people's eyes. Is there no reality in the penitence thus sealed and witnessed by good works? And wherefore should it not bring you peace?' " (190). Hetty would continue an existence that ignores the way "men's lives are as thoroughly blended with each other as the air they breathe" (355) and go on being "one of those numerous people who have had godfathers and godmothers, learned their catechism, been confirmed, and gone to church every Sunday, and yet, for any practical result of strength in life, or trust in death, have never appropriated a single Christian idea or Christian feeling" (321).

For Arthur Dimmesdale and Arthur Donnithorne escape is also a temptation, but in their case a temptation they resist when they publically accept responsibility for their sexual involvement with Hester and Hetty. In *The Scarlet Letter* this matter is crucial from the beginning. The Puritans insist that Hester " 'lay open her heart's secrets' " (66), and even for the "kind and genial" Reverend John Wilson, the only problem is, as he tells Hester, " 'what arguments to use, whether of tenderness or terror, such as might prevail over your hardness and obstinacy; insomuch that you should no longer hide the name of him who tempted you to this grievous fall' " (66). In Eliot's novel Arthur Donnithorne's relationship with Hetty is kept a secret from the people of Hayslope because, as Adam notes, " 'It couldn't be made public . . . without her losing her character' " (252). But Arthur's seduction of Hetty cannot remain hidden once she is arrested for child murder, and an angry Adam Bede is as insistent as any Puritan that Arthur be brought to public account: " 'it's right people should know how she was tempted the wrong way. . . . a fine gentleman made love to her, and turned her head wi' notions. . . . I hold him the guiltiest before God' " (346).

When the two Arthurs openly accept blame for their conduct, they, of course, do more than satisfy their critics. They bring an end to the hypocrisy by which they have protected themselves, and they acknowledge their obligations to the women they have loved. Yet beyond this point the public soul-baring of both Arthurs is of limited worth. It is clearly not an end in itself. In *The Scarlet Letter* Hawthorne summarizes the meaning of Dimmesdale's confession with a Sunday school maxim that does not begin to reveal the depth of the latter's tragedy:[14]

> Among many morals which press upon us from the poor minister's miserable experience, we put only this into a sentence:—"Be true! Be true! Be true! Show freely to the world, if not your worst, yet some trait whereby the worst may be inferred!" (257–8)

In *Adam Bede* Arthur Donnithorne appears in Eliot's epilogue as no more than a sadder version of the man Mr. Irwine earlier described as "weak" but not "coldly selfish" (354):

"Why, he's altered and yet not altered. I should ha' known him anywhere.
But his colour's changed, and he looks sadly. . . . But he speaks just the
same, and smiles at me just as he did when he was a lad. It's wonderful
how he's always had just the same sort o' look when he smiles." (448)

What then is a response equal in passion and understanding to
the tragedies surrounding Hester's and Hetty's falls? This is a question that is answered finally not in terms of any single dramatic
action but in terms of the religious transformation that takes place
within Arthur Dimmesdale and Adam Bede.

IV   In order to understand the nature
of this religious transformation, we must remember that Hawthorne's and Eliot's religious beliefs are by no means identical with
Arthur's and Adam's. This distinction is one that is maintained in
both books in a number of ways. In *The Scarlet Letter* Hawthorne is
very skeptical on the subject of the Puritans' and Dimmesdale's
belief in miracles. When the letter A is sighted in the sky on the
night of John Winthrop's death, Hawthorne comments:

> Nothing was more common, in those days, than to interpret all meteoric
> appearances, and other natural phenomena, that occurred with less
> regularity than the rise and set of sun and moon, as so many revelations
> from a supernatural source. . . . We doubt whether any marked event,
> for good or evil, ever befell New England, from its settlement down to
> Revolutionary times, of which the inhabitants had not been previously
> warned by some spectacle of this nature. (153)

In *Adam Bede* George Eliot's description of the religious atmosphere
created by the Methodists is far more critical:

> I cannot pretend that Seth and Dinah were anything less than Methodists
> . . . of a very old-fashioned kind. They believed in present miracles, in
> instantaneous conversions, in revelations by dreams and visions; they
> drew lots, and sought for Divine Guidance by opening the Bible at hazard
> . . . and it is impossible for me to represent their diction as correct, or
> their instruction as liberal. (34)

Eliot's description of the Methodists does not fully apply to Adam, who is Church of England, but it does include him to the degree that he believes in his wife's "sperrit" and "gift" for preaching (449) and has a "peasant" faith of his own in "dreams and prognostics" (44).

Even more telling is the way Hawthorne and Eliot withhold approval from their principal characters. In *The Scarlet Letter*, for example, it is significant that Hawthorne himself never says that Dimmesdale's confession is a sign of "God's judgment" (253). We have only Dimmesdale's word on this matter, and it is the word of a man about whom Hawthorne previously observed, "the framework of his order inevitably hemmed him in" (199). Similarly, in *Adam Bede* it is essential to note that, despite George Eliot's approval of Adam's marriage and his belief in workmanship, it is only Adam who goes so far as to say God " 'put' " love " 'into his heart and Dinah's' " (424) and that his carpentry is a reflection of "God's will" (407).

With these distinctions in mind, we are then in a position to see that Arthur's and Adam's religious transformations do not center on dogma or propositional ideas about God, but on matters of the heart. Indeed, at this point a comparison of the two books is especially revealing. For rather than focusing attention on Hawthorne's Christian leanings or Eliot's secular humanism, it draws attention to the overriding concern in *The Scarlet Letter* and *Adam Bede* with redemptive knowledge: specifically, with the way Arthur and Adam respond to a fall analogous to that of Adam and Eve and come not only to see their old selves differently but to affirm those very beliefs the fall puts into jeopardy.[15]

The changes in Arthur and Adam do not have their origin in the piety so much as in the conventionality of both men. Arthur has, as Hawthorne notes, been "trammeled" by Puritan society, "by its regulations, its principles, and even its prejudices" (199). One of the main reasons he cannot properly respond to the crisis he faces is that he "had never gone through an experience calculated to lead him beyond the scope of generally received laws" (198–9). In this respect Adam is very similar. It is because he has a "nature, which inclined him to admit all established claims unless he saw very clear grounds for questioning them," (140) that he looks upon his life

prior to Hetty's trial as a "dim sleepy existence" (357). For Arthur
and Adam, the first stage in their transformation, thus, consists of
reaching an acutely pained awareness of their limitations. In both
books the ordeal of reaching this awareness is described in terms of
fire imagery. Dimmesdale speaks of being saved as a result of his
"burning torture" (254):

> "[God] hath proved his mercy, most of all, in my affliction. By giving me
> this burning torture to bear upon my breast! By sending yonder dark and
> terrible old man, to keep the torture always at red-heat! . . . Had either
> of these agonies been wanting, I had been lost for ever!" (254)

Adam's "baptism of fire" (357) is analyzed in parallel terms by
George Eliot:

> Deep, unspeakable suffering may well be called a baptism, a regenera-
> tion, the initiation into a new state. The yearning memories, the bitter
> regret, the agonized sympathy . . . may do the work of years. . . . (357)

For Arthur's and Adam's suffering to be efficacious—for them, in
T. S. Eliot's words, "to be redeemed from fire by fire"—they must,
however, go beyond suffering. Hawthorne's and Eliot's judgment of
human nature was much too tough-minded for them to maintain
that pain alone could renew life. Accordingly, the second stage of
Arthur's and Adam's religious transformations begins only when
they actively reject their past ways of life. Dimmesdale denies the
value of the compromise by which he has lived his life when he tells
Hester, " 'There is no substance in it! It is cold and dead, and can
do nothing for me! Of penance I have had enough! Of penitence
there has been none!' " (190). Adam is equally unsparing of himself
when he asserts, " 'We hand folks over to God's mercy and show
none ourselves' " (360). For his assertion is based on his discovery
that it "seemed to him as if he had always before thought it a light
thing that men should suffer; as if all that he had himself endured
and called sorrow before, was only a moment's stroke that had never
left a bruise" (357). But even at this point Arthur and Adam are still
not free from serious inconsistencies. Arthur temporarily makes
plans to escape to "the Old World with its crowds and cities" (213),
and during his second meeting in the woods with Arthur Donni-

thorne, Adam is unable to prevent "his old severity returning" (390).

Yet once Arthur and Adam do change course, the change is permanent. In theological terms the final stage of their religious transformations is reflected in a total willingness to subordinate their desires to those of a higher power. When Hester asks Dimmesdale if they will ever meet again, his reply is that she is not focusing on ultimate concerns. " 'The law we broke! . . . let these alone be in thy thoughts! . . . Praised be his name! His will be done!' " (254). Adam's proposes to Dinah by telling her, " 'I love you next to the God who made me' " (423). But more importantly, when Dinah is unsure of whether or not it would be right for her to marry, Adam also yields to her judgment that " 'we must submit ourselves entirely to the Divine Will' " (426).

The depth of Arthur's and Adam's religious transformations are, however, most significantly revealed by their responding to Hester's and Hetty's falls with such an abiding sense of their own fallibility that their despair becomes a creative force; one that gives them a new capacity for forming spiritual bonds with others and establishes the original sin in *The Scarlet Letter* and *Adam Bede* as unifying, not merely divisive. The Arthur Dimmesdale who delivers the election-day sermon is so different from the man in the woods that Hester "hardly knew him now" (238). His words cannot be reproduced, but are communicated "in a tongue native to the human heart, wherever educated" (241-2):

> The complaint of a human heart, sorrow-laden, perchance guilty, telling its secret, whether of guilt or sorrow, to the great heart of mankind; beseeching its sympathy or forgiveness,—at every moment,—in each accent,—and never in vain! It was this profound and continual undertone that gave the clergyman his most appropriate power. (242)

Adam Bede's "initiation into a new state" (357) is equally profound, and there is no mistaking George Eliot's approval of the "growing tenderness which came from the sorrow at work within him" (407):

> Let us rather be thankful that our sorrow lives in us as an indestructable force, only changing its form, as forces do, and passing from pain into

sympathy—the one poor word which includes all our best insight and our best love. . . . For it is at such periods that the sense of our lives having visible and invisible relations beyond any of which our present or prospective self is the centre, grows like a muscle we are obliged to lean on and exert. (407)

Indeed, at no other point is the writing in *The Scarlet Letter* and *Adam Bede* more similar, and at no other point is it more logical that it should be. For the vision revealed here is one to which both books build: a vision that explains why it is possible to say of George Eliot, as Hyatt Waggoner has said of Nathaniel Hawthorne, "Over and over again he retold the story of the Fall, and now and then he managed to imagine its sequel, the redemption effected by the Second Adam. Loss of innocence compelled his imagination. . . . The light, whether from the heart or from above, had to be searched out and affirmed as real, just because it was not immediately 'given,' like the darkness."[16]

V   It is not until we turn to the final implications of the fall in *The Scarlet Letter* and *Adam Bede* that the differences in Hawthorne's and Eliot's religious visions become a crucial question. The nature of these differences can be seen with particular clarity in their personal writing. As the following passage from Hawthorne's *English Notebooks* shows, questions of eschatology were of deep concern to him: "God himself cannot compensate us for being born, in any period short of eternity. All the misery we endure here constitutes a claim for another life . . . still more, all the happiness, because all true happiness involves something more than a mortal capacity for the enjoyment of it."[17] For Eliot, on the other hand, although it was impossible to have "antagonism towards any faith in which human sorrow and human longing for purity have expressed themselves," it was, as she wrote D'Albert-Durade, this world and not eternity to which she thought religious concern should be directed: "On that question of future existence . . . my most rooted conviction is that the immediate object and proper sphere of all our highest emotions are our fellow-men in this earthly existence."[18] These same kinds of differences are brought to a head by the structure of *The Scarlet Letter* and *Adam Bede*. Of ultimate importance in *The Scarlet Letter* is what Herbert Read has called in Hawthorne the "almost giddy vertiginous gulf between human finiteness and the affinity of the absolute."[19] In *Adam Bede* such tension is not paramount. Eliot's final and dominant emphasis is on the communal implications of Adam's religious growth.

In *The Scarlet Letter* the problem of bridging the "gulf" that Herbert Read speaks of is foreshadowed as early as the "Custom House" introduction in which Hawthorne describes the difficulty of comprehending the meaning of Hester's letter:

> My eyes fastened themselves upon the old scarlet letter, and would not be turned aside. Certainly, there was some deep meaning in it, most worthy of interpretation, and which, as it were, streamed from the mystic symbol, subtly communicating itself to my sensibilities, but evading the analysis of my mind. (34)

These difficulties in comprehension increase as the letter (with its implication of the fall) is seen or reported on Hester's dress "in fine red cloth, surrounded with an elaborate embroidery" (54), in the sky, "marked out in lines of dull red light" (154), and on Dimmesdale's chest as "his own red stigma" (253). They are difficulties that remain unresolved, however, even after the climax of *The Scarlet Letter*. For although Dimmesdale's religious transformation points to his growth and eventual ability to address "the whole human brotherhood in the heart's native language" (140), it still does not reveal if he is saved or if God's will can be known. To quote Alfred Kazin on this dilemma:

> As a storyteller, choosing to represent psychic situations rather than to explain them, Hawthorne found himself suggesting uncertainties where there had always been God's truth, drawing shadows and hinting at abysses where there had always been clarity, straining to find images of . . . the terror that waits in what he called "the dim region beyond the daylight of our perfect consciousness."[20]

When Dimmesdale, who has "stood out from all the earth to put in his plea of guilty at the bar of Eternal Justice" (252), speaks of the letter on his chest as a sign of "God's judgment on a sinner"

(253), the reader can only know that the question of God's will is crucial in *The Scarlet Letter*. All that Hawthorne says of the letter is, "It was revealed. But it were irreverent to describe that revelation" (253). We cannot be sure if this irreverence is because Dimmesdale is pathetically deluded by his faith in the "ghastly miracle" (253), or if the letter is a manifestation of a revelation that cannot be understood in conventional language. Hawthorne deliberately adds to this ambiguity in his concluding chapter with further debate on the letter, which he follows with the observation, "As regarded its origins, there were various explanations, all of which must necessarily have been conjectural. . . . The reader may choose among these theories. We have thrown all the light we could upon the portent" (256). In the end "the light" Hawthorne throws is so dim that it amounts to confirmation of his view, expressed in *Our Old Home*, that the "machinery of Providence" was "unintelligible."[21]

By contrast, Eliot does not pursue questions of eschatology or revelation. In *Adam Bede* the problem of knowing is, despite Eliot's concern with the "sense of that Unknown towards which we have sent forth irrepressible cries in our loneliness" (407), finally historical and moral in nature. This emphasis is continually brought out in passages like the following, "The secret of our emotions never lies in the bare object, but in its subtle relation to our own past: no wonder the secret escapes the unsympathizing observer, who might as well put on his spectacles to discern odours" (170). The "sympathizing observer" in *Adam Bede* can perceive what previously escaped his vision, and this is what Adam does. Unlike Dimmesdale, who, in Hester's words, " 'lookest far into eternity' " with " 'bright dying eyes' " (254), Adam concentrates on the here and now. His "dim blurred sight" is removed like a "cataract"; and in him the "growth of higher feeling . . . is like the growth of faculty" (442). The result is that Adam's "fuller life" (442) has its most complete expression in the communion he achieves with others. At the time of Hetty's trial this communion is overtly suggestive of the Last Supper. Bartle Massey asks Adam, " 'Take a bit, then, and another sup, Adam, for the love of me,' " and "Nerved by an active resolution [to sit by Hetty] Adam took a morsel of bread, and drank some wine" (360). By the end of Eliot's novel, however, this same kind of "fellow-feeling" is shown without any such symbolism. The "sense of enlarged being" (442) Adam now possesses is reflected in his daily communion with neighbors and family:

> he was aware that common affection and friendship were more precious to him than they used to be,—that he clung more to his mother and Seth, and had an unspeakable satisfaction in the sight or imagination of any small addition to their happiness. The Poysers, too—hardly three or four days passed but he felt the need of seeing them, and interchanging words and looks of friendliness. . . . (408)

The calm at the end of *Adam Bede,* like the fearful ambiguity at the close of *The Scarlet Letter,* thus marks not only the end of a protracted religious struggle, it distinguishes the implications of that struggle, and in so doing, illuminates Hawthorne's and Eliot's fiction as a whole. One is reminded of why William Dean Howells in discussing Henry James and the rise of the analytical novel should have written, "The art of fiction has, in fact, become a finer art in our day than it was with Dickens and Thackeray. . . . These great men are of the past—they and their methods and interests. . . . The new school derives from Hawthorne and George Eliot rather than any others."[22]

NOTES

1. F. R. Leavis, *Anna Karenina and Other Essays* (New York, 1969), p. 52.

2. The other important influence on *Adam Bede* is Sir Walter Scott's *The Heart of Midlothian,* but as Leavis points out, Scott's moral vision was not adequate for Eliot. Eliot herself is outspoken on the subject and wrote of Scott's life, "The spiritual sleep of that man was awful; he does not in the least betray if he felt anything like a pang of conscience." (*The George Eliot Letters,* ed. Gordon S. Haight, vol. I, [New Haven, 1954], p. 24.)

3. For further comparison of *Adam Bede* and *Madame Bovary* see: Dorothy Van Ghent, *The English Novel: Form and Function* (New York, 1965), pp. 179–80; John Paterson, "Introduction," *Adam Bede* (Boston, 1968), pp. xxi–xxiii.

4. Harry Levin, *The Gates of Horn* (New York, 1966), p. 253.

5. All page references are to the following paperback edition: Nathaniel Hawthorne, *The Scarlet Letter* (Boston: Houghton Mifflin, 1960).

6. All page references are to the following paperback edition: George Eliot, *Adam Bede* (Boston: Houghton Mifflin, 1968).

7. In Chapter XVII of *Adam Bede* George Eliot observes, "It is for this rare precious quality of truthfulness that I delight in many Dutch paintings, which lofty-minded people despise. I find a source of delicious sympathy in these faithful pictures of a monotonous homely existence . . ." (p. 152). Mario Praz also explores this aspect of George Eliot's writing in *The Hero in Eclipse* (New York, 1956), pp. 319–83. Hawthorne's comments on genre painting are contained in a letter to James Fields: "It is a sign, I presume, of a taste still very defective, that I take singular pleasure in the elaborate imitations of Van Mieris, Gerard Dow, and other Dutch wizards . . . who spent weeks and months in turning a foot or two of canvas to a perfect microscopic illusion of some homely scene." (Quoted in F. O. Matthiessen, *The American Renaissance* [New York, 1957], p. 323.)

8. For an analysis of the Puritans and prison worship see: Charles Feidelson, Jr., *"The Scarlet Letter," Hawthorne Centenary Essays*, ed. Roy Harvey Pearce (Columbus, Ohio, 1964), p. 52.

9. For further discussion of the restrictiveness of religion in Hayslope see: Jerome Thale, *The Novels of George Eliot* (New York, 1959), p. 20.

10. The usual view of society in *Adam Bede* is far less critical. See, for example, Ian Gregor and Brian Nichols, *The Moral and the Story* (London, 1962), pp. 13–32.

11. F. O. Matthiessen, *The American Renaissance*, p. 306.

12. Hetty's self-worship is treated in detail in Reva Stump, *Movement and Vision in George Eliot's Novels* (Seattle, 1959), pp. 24–9.

13. The religious implications of an escape like Hester's or Hetty's are discussed in Randall Stewart, *American Literature and Christian Doctrine* (Baton Rouge, 1958), pp. 86–7.

14. Frederick Crews explores this subject in *The Sins of the Fathers: Hawthorne's Psychological Themes* (New York, 1966), p. 153.

15. The change in Arthur and Adam bears a strong resemblance to the kind of conversion experience discussed by William James in *The Varieties of Religious Experience* (New York, 1935), pp. 189–258.

16. Hyatt Waggoner, *Hawthorne: A Critical Study* (Cambridge, 1963), p. 259.

17. Nathaniel Hawthorne, *The English Notebooks*, ed. Randall Stewart (New York, 1941), p. 101.

18. *The George Eliot Letters*, vol. 3, p. 231.

19. Herbert Read, *The Nature of Literature* (New York, 1956), p. 269.

20. Alfred Kazin, "The Ghost Sense," *New York Review of Books*, 11 (October 24, 1968): 26.

21. Nathaniel Hawthorne, *Our Old Home and English Notebooks*, vol. 1 (Boston, 1883), p. 46.

22. By great men of the past Howells also has in mind Richardson, whom he finds prolix, and Fielding, whom he describes as coarse. ("Henry James, Jr.," *William Dean Howells: Representative Selections*, ed. Clara Marburg Kirk and Rudolf Kirk [New York, 1961], p. 353.)

5

Herman Melville and Thomas Hardy

I   In reading Melville's *Pierre* and Hardy's *Jude the Obscure*, it is necessary to avoid the kind of traditional analysis in which "Melville appears just as relentless as Hardy can be in his insistence that his central character must fail, that it is a fatal universe, and that only the most horrible end is possible."[1] For such an analysis distorts the fact that the central concern in both novels is not the concept of fate but the concept of nil.[2] The void Pierre and Jude discover in the midst of relatively ordinary surroundings is similar to that which Conrad's Marlow discovers in the Congo when he realizes "the evanescence of all things." But unlike Marlow, who clings to a sense of duty despite the horror of his knowledge, Pierre and Jude are seekers. There is no belief in the future, no higher, more terrifying insight capable of sustaining Pierre once he acknowledges "the everlasting elusiveness of Truth" (472) or Jude once he admits, " 'the further I get the less sure I am' " (258).[3] By the end of their lives both men are estranged from their families and the land on which they were born, from conventional ambition and from faith in a benignly omniscient God.

The process by which Pierre and Jude reach this state of mind, a state of mind in which suicide becomes the next logical step, is, however, so complex that it cannot be traced to any single event or any narrow circle of events. Even the decision that changes the planned course of their lives, the decision that each of them makes

—at the age of twenty and nineteen respectively—to correct a sexual wrong for which he is not responsible, is serious but ultimately not ruinous. In Pierre's case it means that he must abandon his bride and a life of rural ease. In Jude's case it means that he must give up his initial plans to enter Christminster. Yet both Pierre and Jude find these disappointments endurable. When Pierre decides that the best way to help Isabel Banford (who has convinced him that she is his illegitimate half-sister) is to pretend to marry, he is aware of the "wide sea of trouble into which he was plunged" (122), but he sees his role as creative, " 'Isabel thou art my sister; and I will love thee, and protect thee, ay, and own thee through all. . . . I see thee long weeping, and God demands me for thy comforter' " (91). Similarly, although Jude knows that his marriage to Arabella Donn, who has lied to him about being pregnant, will "cripple him . . . for the rest of a lifetime" (52), he does not reach the conclusion that he is doomed. While separated but still married, he decides that "his plan should be to move onward through good and ill—to avoid morbid sorrow even though he did see ugliness . . . to do good cheerfully —which he had heard to be the philosophy of one Spinoza, might be his own even now" (61).

The destruction of Pierre and Jude occurs, to use Murray Krieger's terminology, because their tragic vision (awareness of the futility of human existence) finally comes to dominate their sense of tragedy (awareness of such futility sustained by the cathartic knowledge of an order that ultimately restores harmony).[4] It is this feeling of void or purposelessness that causes Pierre and Jude to see their lives with Kierkegaardian despair and at moments use language similar to his. When Pierre is asked, " 'Are you sick?' " and answers, " 'To death!' " (257), he implies all that Jude does when he says, " 'And what I appear, a sick and poor man, is not the worst of me' " (258). The logic of this despair is revealed in the structure of both books, which centers on three basic concerns: Pierre's and Jude's encounters with a society impervious to their virtues and ambitions, the impossibility of their finding a compromise that does not vitiate all they stand for, and the indifference of nature, as well as any higher power, to their happiness.

II   The society in which Pierre and
Jude find themselves provides the most immediate obstacle to their
happiness, and at times both generalize upon its wrongs. Pierre
speaks of man having been "socially educated for thousands of
years in an arbitrary homage to the Law" (466–7), and Jude asserts
that there is " 'something wrong somewhere in our social for-
mulas' " (259). Yet the social evils that Pierre and Jude attack can
be fully understood only when we realize that Melville's and Hardy's
social criticism is essentially religious and that it depends less on
their development of formal arguments than on their use of style.
In both novels Christian symbolism is used to reveal not only deeply
rooted social hypocrisies but the genuinely religious temper of
Pierre and Jude.

For Pierre and Jude, it is innocence and a willingness to commit
themselves to a higher truth that shapes their earliest religious
feelings. At the start of Melville's novel Pierre is, as Lawrance
Thompson has noted, "surrounded by love, in an Eden-like world,
and repeated analogies are overtly made to suggest that he is as
pure and innocent as Adam before the fall."[5] His "green and golden
world" (1) is so blissful that even his love for Lucy, his fiancée and
an Eve before the fall, is without sex. Only when Isabel, his half-
sister and a highly sensual Eve, enters his life does Pierre stray from
his earthly paradise in Saddle Meadows and begin a different quest.
If Pierre's sexual and worldly innocence seems unusual, it is certainly no more so than Jude's. Until the age of nineteen, when he
meets Arabella, Jude "had never looked at a woman to consider her
as such, but had vaguely regarded the sex as beings outside his life
and purposes" (34). As a result of his involvement with Arabella,
Jude loses his sexual innocence, but this loss (and his disillusionment with Arabella) is no more significant than his awareness that
it is his Adamic vision (of there being enough on earth to feed man
and the animals) that causes him to be dismissed from his first job,
chasing birds from a wheat field. Both these incidents are complementary and help explain why Jude is so anxious to get to Christminster, where he believes the "tree of knowledge grows" (22).

Closely related to but complicating Pierre's and Jude's Adamic
innocence are their Christ-like qualities. In Pierre's case the Christ

imagery is explicit, although it does not, as Henry A. Murray has warned, suggest that Pierre is Christ in modern dress or even an ideal Christian.[6] What it does do, however, is strongly identify features of Pierre's life and aspirations with those of Jesus. We quickly learn that Pierre's earthly mother is named Mary, his dead father, whom Pierre worships in a "shrine," is a figure remembered as "without blemish, unclouded, snowwhite, and serene" (93), and the land on which Pierre was born dates back to the three Indian Kings, who are compared to the Three Magi in the Bible (14). Moreover, Pierre himself speaks of the "Christ-like feeling" (150) he has about his undertaking on Isabel's behalf, and in terms of the intensity with which he defends her, the analogy is valid. As Melville notes, "in the Enthusiast to Duty the heaven-begotten Christ is born; and will not own a mortal parent, and spurns and rends all mortal bonds" (149). In Jude's case his otherworldliness is described in terms of a series of religious references. Sue compares him to "St. Stephen, who, while they were stoning him, could see Heaven opened" and to "Joseph, the dreamer of dreams" (162). He is also, as Frederick P. W. McDowell has shown, similar to Jude, the New Testament scribe, who sought to reclaim his contemporaries to the love of God, and to St. Paul, who returned to Lystra to preach much in the same way that Jude returns to Christminster on Remembrance Day.[7] Finally, Jude refers to himself as a "poor Christ" (100), calls Christminster his "Heavenly Jerusalem" (18), and is Christ-like in his capacity for sacrifice. When he thinks of entering the Church without going to the University, he hopes to "mark out his coming years so as to begin his ministry at the age of thirty—an age which much attracted him as being that of his exemplar when he first began to teach in Galilee" (103).

In contrast to these religious associations are those used to describe the life Pierre and Jude actually find when they move to the city. The references in *Pierre* to Dante's *Inferno* are numerous, especially with regard to New York, which resembles the City of Dis.[8] In New York Pierre's insolent hack driver is compared to the "Charon ferry-men" (324), the first woman he meets is a "scarlet-cheeked, glaringly arrayed" prostitute (331), emblematic of the whore of Babylon, and in the watch house, where he leaves Isabel and Delly

Ulver, he witnesses a scene that suggests to him the "infernoes of hell" (336). In *Jude the Obscure,* the city of Christminster, which Jude initially sees with a "halo" about it (20), also comes to seem like " 'an infernal cursed place' " (260). Jude is jeeringly called the " 'Tutor of St. Slums' " (257) by his fellow workmen and is barred from a life of scholarship by Christminster University, which from his point of view has little to do with Christ or ministers. When Jude's son commits suicide and murder at Christminster, it is the culmination of all the agonies Jude has experienced there. We can only interpret ironically the organ music Jude hears coming from the College Chapel at this point: "Truly God is loving unto Israel" (267).

This negative use of religious associations in the two books is heightened by a parallel use of architecture. Pierre finds that the building he is living in was once used for religious purposes. But the Church of the Apostles has "had its days of sanctification and grace" (370). The church is now "divided into stores; cut into offices; and given for a roost to the gregarious lawyers" (370). The annex in which Pierre is staying has been taken over by "strange nondescript adventurers and artists. . . . Teleological Theorists, and Social Reformers, and political propagandists of all manner of heterodoxical tenets" (374).[9] Thus, money changers, in the form of modern businessmen, have literally entered the church, and religious seriousness has been replaced by reformist impulses Melville can only regard satirically. From his window Pierre notes the "gray and grand old tower" of the "ancient church" (378), but elsewhere he finds "there is nothing to see but a wilderness of tiles, slate, shingles, and tin . . . wherewith we modern Babylonians replace the fair hanging gardens" (377). The lack of religious spirit Jude encounters is even more forcefully symbolized by architectural changes. Sue remarks that the railway station is now the " 'centre of town life' " and that " 'the Cathedral has had its day' " (107), and Jude, who restores churches for his living, confirms the truth of her observation. When he seeks a job in the work-yard of a Christminster stonecutter, he perceives that "at best only copying, patching,and imitating went on" (68); and later he acknowledges that "mediaevalism was as dead as a fern leaf in a lump of coal . . . other developments were shaping the world around him, in which Gothic architecture and its associations had no place" (68–9).

Melville's and Hardy's religious allusions and symbolic use of architecture do not, of course, preclude other kinds of social observation on their part. It is, for example, significant that in both novels there is a breakdown of traditional economic institutions as well as religious ones. Pierre, who has been raised on land still run like an eighteenth-century Dutch estate, finds that in New York, his aristocratic past is a handicap when it comes to earning a living. It is Charlie Millthorpe, whose father once tilled Glendinning land but who himself left the country to settle in the bohemian section of the city, who must help Pierre find rooms and at one point pay some of his debts. Jude has no aristocratic past to fall from, but the work he does, restoring old churches, puts him in an ambivalent situation. His skill is a traditional one, but the way in which he is paid (hiring himself out for wages) points to the future as does the fact that he finds less and less demand for ecclesiastical work.[10] The intensity of Melville's and Hardy's religious concerns is, however, such that social observations like these are absorbed into a larger framework in which the following consequences are most important: 1) the indifference of society to virtually all questions of ultimate truth; 2) the meaning, particularly in an urban setting, of a collective absence of charity; 3) the inefficacy of any sacrificial gesture in a society in which the first two conditions prevail.

Melville's and Hardy's attack on the failure of the societies they were describing to be concerned with anything more than superficial truths is reflected in their attack on the publishing world and the university system. Pierre's wish to write a book is motivated by "the burning desire to deliver what he thought to be a new, or at least miserably neglected Truth to the world" (394) and is similar in its idealism to Jude's desire for an education that will enable him to contribute "his units of work to the general progress of his generation" (52). Both ambitions are met by snobbery and intellectual genteelism, and in each case the final blow comes in the form of a letter. From his publishers, Steel, Flint, and Asbestos, Pierre receives the following communication, " 'You are a swindler. Upon the pretense of writing a popular novel for us, you have been receiving cash advances from us, while passing through our press the sheets of a blasphemous rhapsody. . . . our lawyer . . . is instructed to proceed with instant rigour' "(497). From T. Tetuphenay, Master of Biblioll College, Jude receives a letter that concludes, " 'judging from your description of yourself as a working-man, I venture to think that you will have a much better chance of success in life by remaining in your own sphere and sticking to your trade than by adopting any other course. That, therefore, is what I advise you to do' " (94). In neither situation is the validity of what Pierre and Jude are attempting seriously considered (although certainly with Pierre's novel there is ample reason to believe that it merits criticism). As the tone of both letters makes clear, all their senders care about is preserving the status quo.

A second and equally important matter is the absence of charity that Pierre and Jude experience in New York and Christminster. Pierre uses the streets to exemplify the coldness of New York: " 'Milk dropped from the milkman's can in December, freezes not more quickly on those stones, than does snow-white innocence, if in poverty it chance to fall in these streets' " (321). Jude laments the same condition in Christminster by describing its street lights: "those lamps which had sent into the sky the gleam and glory that caught his strained gaze in his days of dreaming. . . . winked their yellow eyes at him dubiously . . . they did not much want him now" (63). Soon after moving to the city, Pierre and Jude are in fact overwhelmed by the sense of being what David Reisman has called lonely in a crowd.[11] For Pierre, whose life at Saddle Meadows was both socially active and highly structured, this experience is particularly trying. "One in a city of hundreds of thousands of human beings, Pierre was solitary as at the Pole" (471). But even Jude, who was an orphan in Marygreen, finds that in the city he is made to feel "the isolation of his own personality" to such a degree that he comes to regard himself as "one who walked but could not make himself seen or heard" (64).

The degree to which Pierre and Jude are trapped by the lack of ultimate concern and charity in the societies in which they are living is most dramatically revealed by the suicides that occur near the end of both stories. In each book suicide is used to suggest crucifixion. As Lawrance Thompson has noted, in leaving his apartment for the last time, Pierre "passes [Lucy and Isabel] the two Angels—the two thieves—so closely associated with his cumulative crucifixions," and "just after he closes the door, Pierre assumes a tableau position of outstretched arms, like that of Christ on the cross."[12] This fatal arrangement of the three is repeated, without the "outstretched arms" (499), in jail, where Pierre, Lucy, and Isabel die within minutes of each other. A similar scene occurs in *Jude the Obscure* when Jude's son, Father Time, kills himself and the other Fawley children. The three hanging figures, two of them anonymous, are dominated by Father Time, whose coming was previously referred to as an "advent" (221) and who has been described as an "enslaved and dwarfed Divinity" (218). The sign "Jesus Nazarenus Rex Judaeorum" is changed by Father Time himself to a pathetic " 'Done because we are too menny' " (266).[13]

In Melville's novel, as in Hardy's, the nature of society is such that a crucifixion can lead only to a futile sacrifice of life. " 'All's o'er, and ye know him not!' " (505) are Isabel's final words on Pierre's death. Her assertion, which "came gasping from the wall" (505), reflects how trapped Pierre is by a social order in which people do not cry for one another and where the final line of social defense is a wall on which (as if in parody of human tears) "the stone cheeks . . . were trickling" (502). Isabel's belief that neither Pierre's true motives nor his anguish can be understood by those who outlive him is similar in its pessimism to the mood created by the doctor of Father Time. The doctor, who is the most intelligent representative of society to appear in Hardy's novel, can only say " 'there are such boys springing up amongst us—boys of a sort unknown in the last generation —the outcome of new views of life. . . . the beginning of the coming universal wish not to live' " (266). But the doctor can give "no consolation" (266), and in the end it is Jude's landlady (a figure similar to Pierre's turnkey in her indifference to suffering) who reflects societal understanding of the deaths that have taken place.

III   The significance of Pierre's and
Jude's social failures becomes even more important in view of their
awareness that they could have avoided most of their troubles by
making compromises. Pierre speaks of the ease with which he might
have gone on as he was, " 'Had I been heartless now, disowned and
spurningly portioned off the girl at Saddle Meadows, then had I
been happy through a long life on earth . . .' " (502). From the
incident of Delly Ulver, who is banished from Saddle Meadows for
having a child out of wedlock, Pierre knows that neither his mother
nor his neighbors would object to him ignoring his half-sister. He
can be as sure of their approval for his non-action as Jude can be
certain that most of the people in his life will applaud him for
following " 'uncritically the track he finds himself in, without considering his aptness for it' " (258). As Jude observes, the social
system is designed to function without regard for personal worth.
" 'It takes two or three generations to do what I tried to do in one;
and my impulses . . . were too strong not to hamper a man without
advantages' " (258).

Pierre and Jude are also aware that there may be a certain logic
in compromising with society. As a young man, Pierre constantly
has the idea of virtuous expediency thrust before him by the Reverend Mr. Falsegrave, whose views are symbolized by his "cameo
brooch, representing the allegorical union of the serpent and dove"
(143). More importantly, on his way to the city Pierre reads Plotinus
Plinlimmon's pamphlet, which advises against mankind trying to act
in accord with the Sermon on the Mount:

> "Though Christ encountered woe in both the precept and the practice
> of his chronometricals, yet did he remain throughout entirely without
> folly or sin. Whereas, almost invariably, with inferior beings, the absolute
> effort to live in this world according to the strict letter of the chronomet-
> ricals is, somehow, apt to involve these inferior beings eventually in
> strange, *unique* follies and sins, unimagined before." (296)

The voice of compromise in Jude's life is his former teacher Richard
Phillotson, who, as his name implies, has the character of a Philis-
tine.[14] A man who, like Jude, has wished for a university education
and been in love with Sue, Phillotson comes to assert, " 'Cruelty is

the law pervading all nature and society; and we can't get out of it if we would!' " (252). He believes that his life has been threatened with "disastrous failure" through his "acting on what he considered at the time a principle of justice, charity, and reason" (284), and he reverses himself in order to regain some of his former tranquility:

> To indulge one's instinctive and uncontrolled sense of justice and right was not, he had found, permitted with impunity in an old civilization like ours. It was necessary to act under an acquired and cultivated sense of the same, if you wished to enjoy an average share of comfort and honour; and to let crude loving-kindness take care of itself. (285)

Pierre's and Jude's awareness of the risks in what they are doing is not sufficient, however, to end their hatred of all that compromise involves. Early in his life Pierre vows to "forsake the censuses of men, and seek the suffrages of the god-like population of the trees" (150), and at no time does he betray this desire to overcome "the detested and distorted images of all the convenient lies and duty-subterfuges of the diving and ducking moralities of this earth" (150). Jude's protests are less bombastic than Pierre's but no less intense. He is aware that he " 'should be as cold-blooded as a fish and as selfish as a pig to have a really good chance of being one of his country's worthies' " (258), and he refuses to be so. Particularly in his relations with Arabella and Sue, Jude carries his kindness to the point of self-destruction. " 'I am not,' " he tells Arabella, " 'a man who wants to save himself at the expense of the weaker among us' " (303).

The question that remains then is: Given Pierre's and Jude's awareness of the perils in what they are doing and the reasons for not doing it, what causes their final disillusionment? The obvious answer would seem to be their realization of their own limitations. Certainly both speak of the subconscious and demeaning motives that are part of their actions. Pierre recognizes that his defense of Isabel has a latent sexual element to it:

> he was assured that, in a transcendent degree, womanly beauty and not womanly ugliness, invited him to champion the right. . . . How [would he have acted] if accosted in some squalid lane, a humped, and crippled,

> hideous girl should have snatched his garment's hem with—"Save me,
> Pierre—love me, own me, brother, I am thy sister!" (151)

Jude is equally certain that his desire for an education contains a
strong measure of self-seeking:

> The old fancy which had led on to the culminating vision of the bishropic
> had not been an ethical or theological enthusiasm at all, but a mundane
> ambition masquerading in a surplice. He feared that his whole scheme
> had degenerated to, even though it might not have originated in, a social
> unrest which had no foundation in the nobler instincts; which was purely
> an artificial product of civilization. (102)

Yet neither Pierre nor Jude is deterred by these shocks of recognition. They are destroyed by their loss of faith in the existence of an
order that, although it might not benefit them, would at least justify
their actions and their suffering.

IV   The importance of this order is
reflected in the fact that Pierre and Jude have based their lives on
there being a correspondence between their moral conduct and a
higher truth. Once this higher truth seems undiscoverable or
nonexistent, the same emptiness applies—as far as they are concerned—to their own lives. It is, however, as a result of a pattern of
fatal discoveries, not merely an isolated experience or two, that
Pierre and Jude reach such a conclusion, and their final despair must
be described in terms of a philosophic whole rather than a sequence
of events.

In this light the most obvious fact about the world in which Pierre
and Jude are living is that it lacks harmony. The practical and the
beautiful, the human and the natural are out of phase, and in both
novels this conflict is revealed in the contradictions nature poses for
men trying to make a living from the land. On Pierre's estate the
"terraced pastures grow glittering white, and in warm June still
show like banks of snow" (477). Yet this beauty is the bane of the
Glendinning tenants, for its source is "a small white amaranthine
flower, which, being irreconcilably distasteful to the cattle, and
wholly rejected by them, and yet continually multiplying on every

hand, did by no means contribute to the agricultural values of these elevated lands" (477). To make their "disheartened dairy tenants" (477) happy the Glendinnings must either reduce their rent or destroy the beauty of the land. In this unpleasant choice they face the same kind of problem that Jude does when he is paid for chasing crows from Farmer Troutham's wheat field. For although Jude believes there is enough seed for all, he must still acknowledge his "perception of the flaw in the terrestrial scheme, by which what was good for God's birds was bad for God's gardener" (15). Jude is fired for not doing his job, but his basic worry remains, "Events did not rhyme quite as he had thought. Nature's logic was too horrid to care for. That mercy towards one set of creatures was cruelty towards another sickened his sense of harmony" (17).

Any Emersonian theory of compensation that might be found to minimize this situation is undercut by both Melville and Hardy in direct comments to the reader and never used by Pierre and Jude to ease their personal burdens. As Melville notes, "Say what some poets will, Nature is not so much her own ever-sweet interpreter, as the mere supplier of that cunning alphabet, whereby selecting and combining as he pleases, each man reads his own peculiar lesson according to his own peculiar mind and mood" (476). Hardy comments on the same ambiguous potential in nature when he observes of Sue's belief that "the world . . . was wonderfully excellent to the half-aroused intelligence, but hopelessly absurd at the full waking": "But affliction makes opposing forces loom anthropomorphous, and those ideas were now exchanged for a sense of Jude and herself fleeing from a persecutor" (271). In both novels the element that most aptly characterizes nature is mist. It is on a "misty eve" (153) that Pierre has his first meeting with Isabel and discovers "a world inhospitable" (153) and it is mist that clouds Pierre's vision when he thinks of his past and Lucy, whom he can only glimpse "half veiled in the lower mist" (147). In Hardy's novel mist appears less frequently. Yet it is a "thinning mist" that prevents Jude from seeing Christminster (19), and it is mist that also increases his feelings of loneliness. "The brown surface of the field . . . was lost by degrees in the mist that shut out the verge and accentuated the solitude" (13).

The mist that Pierre and Jude can never fully penetrate would not be such an obstacle, however, if there were some metaphysical hope they might cling to. Yet as both discover, the Gods are no more concerned about them than is nature. Pierre learns, "Silence is at once the most harmless and the most awful thing in all nature. . . . Silence is the only Voice of our God" (284). But even before he arrives at this view, Pierre admits to himself that "all the world, and every misconcievably common and prosaic thing in it, was steeped a million fathoms in a mysteriousness wholly hopeless of solution" (180). Jude's inability to discover any higher truth is no less apparent, and his confusion, like that of Pierre, leaves him without hope:

> "I am in a chaos of principles—groping in the dark—acting by instinct and not after example. Eight or nine years ago . . . I had a neat stock of fixed opinions, but they dropped away one by one; and the further I get the less sure I am . . . 'For who knoweth what is good for a man in this life?—and who can tell a man what shall be after him under the sun?' "
> (258–9)

Under these circumstances the fact that Pierre and Jude have not acted in accord with their natural instincts is especially serious, for it means there remains nothing tangible to compensate them for the sacrifices they have made. The sexual frustrations of Pierre and Jude are, for example, never resolved or sublimated. Pierre is unable to achieve any sexual union with the "nun-like" (436) Lucy, whom he loves but gives up, and his attraction to Isabel, upon whom he presses "repeated burning kisses" (268), is guilt-ridden and incestuous. Jude is equally unfortunate.[15] He idealizes Sue, who, like Lucy, is an "aerial being" (171), but he idealizes her to such a degree that he accedes to her frigid sexual request " 'to set my wishes above your gratification' " (190). Moreover, while Jude has a strong sexual response to Arabella, who is described by Hardy as "a complete and substantial female animal" (33), his own aspirations turn him away from her coarseness, and they are never happy together.

To make matters worse, Pierre and Jude cannot confine the consequences of their actions to their own lives, and unavoidably they bring suffering upon their families. Pierre goes so far as to blame himself for the premature death of his mother, who does in fact change after she learns of his plans to marry Isabel. "Pierre cursed himself for a heartless villain and an idiot fool—heartless villain as the murderer of his own mother—idiot fool because he had thrown away all his felicity . . . for a mess of pottage, which now proved all but ashes in his mouth" (403). Jude does not see himself as the direct cause of Father Time's suicide, but he nonetheless regards his aspirations as the source of the whole circle of misery in which he and his family are trapped, " 'I have seemed to myself lately . . . to belong to that vast band of men shunned by the virtuous —the men called seducers. It amazes me when I think of it! . . . Yet, I *am* one of those men! I wonder if any other of them are the same purblind, simple creatures as I?' " (271).

So pointless is the suffering Pierre and Jude feel they have caused, that by the end of their lives no intellectual or religious belief can sustain them. Melville carefully notes the destruction of Pierre's "high-wrought, stoic, and philosophic defences" (403):

> For there is no faith, and no stoicism, and no philosophy, that a mortal man can possibly evoke, which will stand the final test of a real impassioned onset of Life and Passion upon him. Then all the fair philosophic or Faith-phantoms that he raised from the mist slide away and disappear as ghosts at cock-crow. (403)

On one of his last walks through the colleges at Christminster, Jude makes a similar comment about his own predicament, " 'The theologians, the apologists, and their kin the metaphysicians, the high-handed statesmen, and others, no longer interest me. All that has been spoilt for me by the grind of stern reality!' " (311). The result is that Pierre and Jude come to see themselves estranged from everything and everyone. Their tragic vision can no longer be modified or made to yield to a principle of tragic catharsis. Pierre believes that he "was utterly without sympathy from anything divine, human, brute, or vegetable" (471), and Jude agrees with Sue that they are made " 'a spectacle unto the world, and to angels, and to men' " (271). Both men, thus, welcome their deaths at the same time they reject the prospect of a new life. Pierre speaks of his "untimely, timely end" as futile: " 'Life's last chapter well-stitched in the middle! Nor book, nor author of the book, hath any sequel, though each hath its last lettering! It is ambiguous still' " (502). Jude's apotheosis is equally bitter. With the sounds from the Remembrance Day games at Christminster coming through his bedroom window, his final words are a repeat of Job's terrible curse: "Let the day perish wherein I was born, and the night in which it was said, 'There is a man child conceived' " (321).

There is no darker point in all of Melville's or Hardy's writing than the deaths of Pierre and Jude, and it is not surprising that after this, both writers felt the need to change artistic directions. With more than half his life, nearly forty years, left, Melville's most significant energy would not go into novels but into short fiction and verse. Hardy would abandon fiction altogether and work only on plays and verse in the more than twenty years remaining in his life.

V   Despite these parallels, it is essential not to lose sight of the differences in Pierre and Jude and how they reach fruition by the end of each book. Melville's story stresses the titanic nature of Pierre's rebellion, his desire to "get on some other element than earth" (485). Hardy's narrative, on the other hand, places Jude in a perspective in which his day to day suffering is more telling than his defiance of "man and senseless circumstance" (271).[16] This distinction is particularly apparent in the references that Pierre and Jude make to Greek legend. Pierre comes to see himself like the Greek god Enceladus, an incestuous creation of heaven and earth. Near the end of his life he imagines that his "own duplicate face and features" (482) appear on the figure of Enceladus embedded in the hills of the Glendinning estate:

> Such was the wild scenery—the Mount of Titans, and the repulsed group of heaven-assaulters, with Enceladus in their midst . . . which now to Pierre, in his strange vision, displaced the four blank walls, the desk, and campbed, and domineered upon his trance.

Pierre saw Enceladus no more; but on the Titan's armless trunk, his own duplicate face and features magnifiedly gleamed upon him with prophetic discomfiture and woe. (482)

By contrast Jude's most significant reference to Greek legend is to the chorus of Agamemnon, and what his reference reveals are feelings of intense helplessness on his part, " 'Nothing can be done. . . . Things are as they are, and will be brought to their destined issue' " (269).

This difference in perspective, which is evident in the fact that Pierre ends his life by committing suicide and Jude dies as a result of a long and partly self-induced illness, is consistent with the course of both men's lives. In Pierre's case the notion of unyielding defiance is vital to all the decisions he makes. Before leaving Saddle Meadows he asserts, "exiled for eye from God and man, I shall declare myself an equal power with both; free to make war on Night and Day" (150). Later he says of his writing, " 'I fight a duel in which all seconds are forbid' " (486), and when the manuscript on which he has staked his financial and literary hopes is rejected and he must fight an actual duel, Pierre declares, " 'World's bread of life, and world's breath of honour, both are snatched from me; but I defy all world's bread and breath . . . and challenge one and all of them to battle' " (498). In Jude's case the quality of his defiance is much less intense than his sensitivity to trappedness. He continually equates his existence with that of animals who are the victims of a greater and (to the animals) incomprehensible power. "A magic thread of fellow-feeling united his life with theirs. Puny and sorry as those lives were, they much resembled his own" (14), Jude says of the birds in Farmer Troutham's wheat field. As a child, Jude is afraid of walking among earth worms for fear of "killing a single one" (16). In his marriage with Arabella he feels guilty about bleeding a pig, whom he calls a "fellow-mortal" (55), and with Sue he has a similarly pained reaction to a rabbit they find caught in a trap (169). Even at Christminster Jude interprets the beating of a horse as an indication of the state of human progress, " 'If that can be done . . . at college gates in the most religious and educational city in the world, what shall we say as to how far we've got?' " (259).

By the conclusion of *Pierre* and *Jude* Melville and Hardy have carried these differences as far as they will go. Pierre's rebellion finally reflects a timeless confrontation with the absurd,[17] one best seen in light of his vision of Enceladus as:

> the most potent of all the giants, writhing from out the imprisoning earth . . . though armless, resisting with his whole striving trunk, the Pelion and the Ossa hurled back at him . . . still turning his unconquerable front toward that majestic mount eternally in vain assailed by him, and which, when it had stormed him off, had heaved his undoffable incubus upon him, and deridingly left him there to bay out his ineffectual howl. (480)

Jude's suffering reflects what Hardy in a letter to Edmund Gross referred to as the "grimy" features of his story.[18] The most revealing view we have of Jude at the end of his life occurs on his death bed as he "rambled on upon the defeat of his early aims": (317)

> "I was never really stout enough for the stone trade, particularly the fixing. Moving the blocks always used to strain me, and standing the trying draughts in buildings before the windows are in, always gave me colds, and I think that began the mischief inside. But I felt I could do one thing if I had the opportunity. I could accumulate ideas, and impart them to others. . . . I hear that soon there is going to be a better chance for such helpless students as I was. . . . I don't know much about it. And it is too late, too late for me!" (317)

NOTES

1. James Guetti, *The Limits of Metaphor: A Study of Melville, Conrad, and Faulkner* (Ithaca, 1967), p. 134.

2. This concept is treated at length in Robert Adams, *Nil: Episodes in the Literary Conquest of Void During the Nineteenth Century* (New York, 1966).

3. All page references are to the following paperback editions: Herman Melville, *Pierre, or the Ambiguities* (New York: Grove Press, 1957); Thomas Hardy, *Jude the Obscure* (Boston: Houghton Mifflin, 1965).

4. Murray Kreiger, *The Tragic Vision* (Chicago, 1966), pp. 3–14.

5. Lawrance Thompson, *Melville's Quarrel with God* (Princeton, 1966), p. 250.

6. Henry A. Murray, "Introduction," *Pierre* (New York, 1949), pp. lxii-lxiv.

7. Frederick P. W. McDowell, "Hardy's 'Seeming or Personal Impressions': The Symbolic Use of Image and Contrast in 'Jude the Obscure,' " *Modern Fiction Studies* 6 (Autumn 1960): 239–40. See also Michael Millgate, *Thomas Hardy: His Career as a Novelist* (New York, 1971), pp. 328–9.

8. Nathalia Wright, "*Pierre:* Herman Melville's Inferno," *American Literature* 32 (May 1960): 167–81.

9. Melville's analysis of certain reform movements in this period is parallel to the analysis of Gilbert Seldes in *Stammering Century* (New York, 1956), pp. 3–13.

10. Irving Howe treats this question of wages in *Thomas Hardy* (New York, 1967), p. 137.

11. David Riesman, *The Lonely Crowd* (Garden City, 1953), pp. 19–48.

12. Lawrance Thompson, *Melville's Quarrel with God*, p. 290.

13. There is good reason for seeing "menny" as a macabre pun, meaning like men, rather than as a colloquialism for many. Walter K. Gordon, "Father Time's Suicide Note in *Jude the Obscure,*" *Nineteenth Century Fiction* 22 (December 1967): 298–9.

14. The symbolism of Phillotson's name is explored in detail by Norman Holland, Jr., " 'Jude the Obscure': Hardy's Symbolic Indictment of Christianity," *Nineteenth Century Fiction* 9 (June 1954): 51.

15. The implications of Jude's divided sexual life are treated in A. Alvarez, "*Jude the Obscure,*" *Hardy*, ed. Albert Guerard (Englewood Cliffs, 1963), pp. 116–19.

16. Melville's concern with Titanism is given detailed analysis in Merlin Bowen, *The Long Encounter* (Chicago, 1963), pp. 128–97. For further treatment of the mythology in *Pierre* see: H. Bruce Franklin, *The Wake of the Gods: Melville's Mythology* (Stanford, 1963), pp. 99–125.

17. Camus's definition of the absurd as "born of this confrontation between the human need and the unreasonable silence of the world" is especially relevant here. (*The Myth of Sisyphus and Other Essays* [New York, 1959], p. 21.)

18. Quoted in Michael Millgate, *Thomas Hardy: His Career as a Novelist*, p. 326.

6

Charles Dickens and Mark Twain

I   With the exception of Sir Walter
Scott and Fenimore Cooper, no English and American writers of the
nineteenth century seem more suited for comparison than Charles
Dickens and Mark Twain. Yet the analyses we have of their work are,
in general, very limited. Why should this be the case? There are, I
think, two basic reasons. The first is that Twain's comments on
Dickens discourage a comparison of the two. If, for a modern critic
like Ellen Moers, it is clear that Twain resembled Dickens in "the
theatricality of his prose, the conception of the public as an audience
of responsive listeners rather than as solitary readers, the episodic
nature of his fiction cut to an oral rather than a literary measure,"
to Twain himself it seemed unnecessary to make such an acknowledgment.[1] In his fiction, as well as in his correspondence, Dickens's
specific influence is at best marginal,[2] and in his *Autobiography* the
latter is relegated to the position of the artist-innovator of the public
reading:

> What is called a "reading," as a public platform entertainment, was first
> essayed by Charles Dickens, I think. He brought the idea with him from
> England in 1867. He had made it very popular at home and he made it
> so acceptable and so popular in America that the houses were crowded
> everywhere, and in a single season he earned two hundred thousand
> dollars.

Dickens had set a fashion which others tried to follow, but I do not remember that anyone was any more than temporarily successful in it. The public reading was discarded after a time and was not resumed until something more than twenty years after Dickens had introduced it; then it rose and struggled along for a while in that curious and artless industry called Authors' Readings.[3]

The second and more important reason for the limited comparative understanding we have of Dickens and Twain lies in the ease with which it is possible to classify the similarities in their fiction as comic. Too often, this observation has provided the conclusion rather than the starting point for an analysis of their writing, and as a result, the degree to which the most important parallels in their work lead in a direction opposite to comedy has been ignored.[4] The point of this statement is not that comedy in Dickens and Twain is a peripheral matter or sugar coating for the naive reader, but that comedy reveals an automatism and insensitivity that Dickens's and Twain's heroes find within themselves and then struggle to overcome.

This development is especially apparent in *Great Expectations* and *Huckleberry Finn*. In both books the fundamental source of comedy (it takes·a variety of secondary forms) is Pip's and Huck's outward allegiance to a society whose values they instinctively oppose. It is this false allegiance that leads Pip to imagine that everything in his environment looks on him with disapproval and causes the voice of Huck's conscience to speak to him in the rhetoric of St. Petersburg. At the beginning of the two stories, whenever Pip and Huck act in conflict with the rules of society and family that have been imposed upon them, their primary feelings are ones of exaggerated guilt. In Pip's case his guilt first emerges when he takes food to the starving convict Abel Magwitch:

> I got up and went downstairs; every board upon the way, and every crack in every board, calling after me, "Stop thief!" and "Get up, Mrs. Joe!" In the pantry . . . I was very much alarmed by a hare hanging up by the heels, whom I rather thought I caught, when my back was half turned, winking. . . . I stole some bread, some rind of cheese, about half a jar of mincemeat. . . . (14)

This was very disagreeable to a guilty mind. The gates of dykes and banks came bursting at me through the mist, as if they cried as plainly as could be, "A boy with Somebody-else's pork pie! Stop him!" (15)[5]

In Huck's case his guilt surfaces when he helps Jim escape from slavery:

> Conscience says to me, "What had poor Miss Watson done to you, that you could see her nigger go off right under your eyes and never say one single word? What did that poor old woman do to you, that you could treat her so mean? Why, she tried to learn you your book, she tried to learn you your manners, she tried to be good to you every way she knowed how." (75)

> Thinks I, this is what comes of my not thinking. Here was this nigger which I had as good as helped to run away, coming right out flat-footed and saying he would steal his children—children that belonged to a man I didn't even know; a man that hadn't ever done me no harm. (75)[6]

As long as this guilt remains the dominant element in their thinking; that is, as long as Pip and Huck view their compassion and rebellion as "criminal," they are bound to be comic figures, guided by the rigid demands of a "deformed conscience" as opposed to the human demands of a "sound heart."[7] It is, however, along lines leading away from this comedy—to a point where Pip and Huck willingly risk their lives to save Magwitch and Jim—that one finds the essential movement of the two stories, and accordingly, it is by focusing on how Pip and Huck translate their deepest feelings into words and actions that we get the fullest picture of Dickens's and Twain's art.

II   Both *Great Expectations* and *Huckleberry Finn* can be divided into three sections: the first dealing with childhood and the home, the second with society as a whole, and the third with the psychological and moral decisions that Pip and Huck reach.[8] The relationship between these sections is dialectical with the natural sympathies of Pip and Huck constituting a thesis, the artificial distinctions of society an antithesis, and the personal responsibilities that Pip and Huck finally assume a synthesis. The only serious modification required of this interpretation is that it allow for the fact that in the first sections of *Great Expectations* and *Huckleberry Finn* the instinctive goodness of Pip and Huck is frequently inhibited or frustrated. This fact is, however, an extremely important one, for in Dickens's and Twain's novels, as in Erik Erikson's *Childhood and Society,* the brutalization of children by adults is not just a psychological matter but a reflection of a much wider system of social custom and exploitation.[9]

For Pip and Huck the problem of growing up absurd begins with the danger posed by homes that offer neither safety nor freedom.[10] Pip comments, "Home had never been a very pleasant place to me, because of my sister's temper" (107), and Huck observes, "it was rough living in the house all the time, considering how dismal regular and decent the widow was in all her ways" (3). The picture of home as a pastoral jail run by women is thoroughly drawn in both novels. In the Gargery household Joe is, as Pip says, "a larger species of child" (7). His domestic function is to earn a living and leave all important decisions to the harsh discretion of Mrs. Joe. As Joe himself admits to Pip, " 'I don't deny that your sister comes the Mo-gul over us, now and again. I don't deny that she do throw us back-falls . . . candour compels fur to admit that she is a Buster' " (48). With the Widow Douglas and Miss Watson tensions between the masculine and the feminine have been eliminated altogether. There are no men in their house, and those men who try to enter their world are, like Pap Finn, driven away. "He got to hanging around the widow's too much, and so she told him at last, that if he didn't quit using around there she would make trouble for him" (21).

In stressing the manner in which women dominated domestic life in mid-nineteenth-century England and America, Dickens and Twain were not, however, guilty of making literary sport of what James Thurber has called "the war between the sexes." As such modern studies as Walter Houghton's *The Victorian Frame of Mind* and William R. Taylor's *Cavalier and Yankee* have shown, the ideal home of the period was one in which the woman ruled supreme in matters of taste and the man devoted himself to material pursuits.[11]

To Dickens's and Twain's credit, they recognized how this arrangement was bound to be inhibiting. Pip and Huck have so many
restrictions placed before them that even the clothes they wear
come to symbolize the way in which their freedom is threatened. Pip
finds that "when I was taken to have a new suit of clothes, the tailor
had orders to make them like a kind of Reformatory, and on no
account to let me have the free use of my limbs" (22). Huck puts
on his "old rags" whenever he leaves the Widow Douglas, but on
returning to her house, he submits to her taste, "She put me in them
new clothes again, and I couldn't do nothing but sweat and sweat,
and feel all cramped up" (3).

The most serious anxiety that Pip and Huck are made to feel is,
however, a consequence of the worn and distorted Calvinism of
their elders. As orphans (Huck does not technically become one
until the middle of his adventures), Pip and Huck must depend
upon the kindness of families that are not their own. By itself this
is not a humiliating necessity. The difficulty lies in the attitudes of
Mrs. Joe, the Widow Douglas, and Miss Watson. Mrs. Joe treats Pip
as if he "had insisted on being born in opposition to the dictates of
reason, religion, and morality" (22). She finds him " 'naterally wi-
cious' " (24), as her friend Mr. Hubble expresses it, and she constantly reminds him of his innate unworthiness by warning him "in
a reproachful voice" to be grateful to those who "brought him up
by hand" (24). The Widow Douglas is constantly crying over Huck
and calling him a "poor lost lamb" (3), but it is Miss Watson who
is hardest on him. She is the one who draws the relationship between Huck's natural feelings and the likelihood of him going to
"the bad place" (4), and it is her version of Hell that torments Huck
when he helps Jim escape. Under these circumstances it is obvious
why Pip and Huck wish to leave the only homes they have known.
What is not obvious and requires close attention is the way in which
their flights from home are given positive shape by the symbolic
rebirths they experience through their involvements with Magwitch
and Jim.

In *Great Expectations* Pip's rebirth occurs in the graveyard in which
his parents and his brothers are buried. The time of the year is
Christmas, and the natural setting is dominated by the slime and

ooze of "the marsh country down by the river" (1). Like a newborn
child, Pip is lifted upside down and held by his heels. The church
steeple he is looking at turns over, and so does his sense of the
world. As he comments, "My first most vivid and broad impression
of the identity of things, seems to me to have been gained on a
memorable and raw afternoon towards evening" (1–2). Although
Huck's rebirth occurs in a natural setting, the mud and water of the
Mississippi, not unlike the scene of Pip's rebirth, the occasion itself
is contrived, for Huck has deliberately staged his own death. "They
won't ever hunt the river for anything but my dead carcass. They'll
soon get tired of that, and won't bother no more about me" (30).
Having drowned, as far as everyone else is concerned, Huck is free
to assume a new identity, and this is what he does at each of his stops
along the river. As James Cox has noted, "The rebirth theme . . .
becomes the driving idea behind the entire action."[12]

The first human contact that Huck has after his escape from his
natural father is with the runaway slave Jim, who will, as Daniel
Hoffman has observed, become his spiritual father and shape his
loyalties in ways that Pap Finn never could.[13] This meeting is as
significant as Pip's upside down encounter with Magwitch, who will
later tell him, " 'Look'ee here, Pip. I'm your second father. You're
my son—more to me nor any son' " (324). The ties binding Pip to
Magwitch and Huck to Jim are the most important indication in both
novels of Dickens's and Twain's belief in the transcendent value of
love. These relationships enable Pip and Huck to distinguish between their false guilt (their failure to conform) and their real guilt
(their failure to accept moral responsibility). The result is that by the
close of the middle sections of *Great Expectations* and *Huckleberry Finn*
Pip and Huck are in a position to realize that their involvement with
society depends on their ability to move beyond the limits of socially
accepted conduct.

III   The middle sections of *Great Ex-*
pectations and *Huckleberry Finn* are less tightly drawn than the other
sections. They are, nonetheless, held together by two related concerns: Dickens's and Twain's criticism of society, and Pip's and

Huck's growing awareness of what people claim to stand for and
what economic and social pressures force them to do. In both novels
these pressures are dramatically symbolized by rivers: specifically,
the swift current and the murky color of the Thames and the Mississippi. Indeed, how similar a purpose the rivers serve is reflected in
descriptions of them by Dorothy Van Ghent and T. S. Eliot. Miss
Van Ghent observes in her critical study, *The English Novel: Form and
Function:*

> The river is perhaps the most constant and effective symbol in Dickens,
> because it establishes itself so readily to the imagination as a daemonic
> element, drowning people as if by intent, disgorging unforeseen evi-
> dence, chemically or physically changing all it touches . . . but it is [also]
> the common passage and actual flowing element that unites individuals
> and classes, public persons and private persons, deeds and results of
> deeds, however fragmentized and separated.[14]

T. S. Eliot writes in his introduction to the Cresset edition of *Huckleberry Finn:*

> The River gives the book its form . . . it runs with a speed such that no
> man or beast can survive in it. At such times, it carries down human
> bodies, cattle and houses.
>
> It is the River that controls the voyage of Huck and Jim . . . it is the River
> that separates them and deposits Huck for a time in the Grangerford
> household; that reunites them, and then compels upon them the unwel-
> come company of the King and the Duke. Recurrently we are reminded
> of its presence and its power.[15]

The rivers in *Great Expectations* and *Huckleberry Finn* are, of course,
finally betrayers. At the moment when they should lead to freedom
they lead to the capture of Magwitch and Jim. Yet such results are
appropriate in terms of the social criticism dominating the middle
sections of both books. The nature of this criticism is no different
from that appearing in the first and final sections of *Great Expectations*
and *Huckleberry Finn,* but it is more detailed, and makes it clear that
in Dickens's and Twain's opinions, the societies they were describing did not possess classes or institutions capable of redeeming
themselves. In each book the dominant image of society is that of

a fallen and virtually forgotten Eden.[16] It is vulgarity, not corruption, that distinguishes the "rank ruin of cabbage-stalks" (80) in Miss Havisham's Old World garden from the New World squalidness of Bricksville, Arkansas, where the "houses had little gardens about them" with nothing but "ash piles" and "old curled-up boots" (117).

The specific differences in the classes and the institutions Dickens and Twain criticize are of secondary importance in comparison with the broader evaluations both authors make of social systems in which the ideal state of affluence is one in which the successful live off the labor of the poor by keeping them in financial, and in some cases physical, subjugation. Thus, Miss Havisham's self-imposed exile illustrates the same kind of social dissolution that the Grangerford-Shepherdson feud does: namely, that of an aristocracy degenerating into a struggle for survival that is hopelessly tied to the past. Satis House, with its rooms "covered with dust and mould, and dropping to pieces" and its "clocks all stopped together" (84), is as devoted to death as the Grangerford home, where the dead Emmeline's room is kept with "all the things fixed in it just the way she liked to have them" (88) and the mantel clock "would start in and strike a hundred and fifty before she got tuckered out" (85). Moreover, Miss Havisham's emotional starvation of Estella has the same psychological consequences as the Grangerford's sentimental indulgence of the poetry-writing Emmeline. It produces a young woman who is obedient to a code of behavior but who has no natural feelings.

Middle class society in *Great Expectations* and *Huckleberry Finn* is similarly disappointing. Its solid citizens, its Uncle Pumblechooks and Judge Thatchers, are at best dull and at worst ingratiating. The source of the admiration these people have for Pip and Huck is the money the boys acquire. Pip, when poor, is tyrannized over by Uncle Pumblechook, who continually tells him to " 'be forever grateful to all friends' " (52). But the moment Pip comes into money, everything changes. He ceases being the boy who on Christmas was given "the scaly tips of the drumsticks of the fowls" and the "corners of pork of which the pig, when living, had had the least reason to be vain" (24). Pumblechook now defers to Pip, "By degrees he fell to reposing such confidence in me, as to ask my advice in reference to his own affairs. . . . What alone was wanting to the realization of a vast fortune, he considered to be More Capital. Those were the two little words, more capital" (157). Huck receives the same kind of treatment. His position in St. Petersburg is a carryover from the time in *Tom Sawyer* when he and Tom "found the money that the robbers hid in the cave, and it made us rich" (3). Prior to that discovery, Huck was, as is clear in *Tom Sawyer,* "cordially hated and dreaded by all the mothers of the town, because he was idle and lawless and vulgar and bad."[17] It is his new fortune that gives him special status and, to cite *Tom Sawyer* again, causes the respectable community to see him in a different light: "The boys were not able to remember that their remarks had possessed weight before; but now their sayings were treasured and repeated; everything they did seemed somehow to be regarded as remarkable. . . ."[18]

It is only in lower class society in *Great Expectations* and *Huckleberry Finn* that the question of status is never the foremost concern, and there is no indication that this situation is due to anything more than a lack of money. Although Dickens and Twain were sensitive to social injustice, the poor in *Great Expectations* and *Huckleberry Finn* are not given credit for possessing any special, collective virtues. Indeed, they murder and exploit each other as readily as they do anyone else. Magwitch, for example, is betrayed not just by Compeyson but, as Orlick indicates, by convicts exiled to Australia, " 'There's them that can't and that won't have Magwitch . . . alive in the same land with them, and that's had such sure information of him when he was alive in another land, as that he couldn't and shouldn't leave it unbeknown and put them in danger' " (435). Similarly, the "loafers" in Bricksville encourage not only the shooting of Boggs but virtually any cruelty: "There couldn't anything wake them up all over, and make them happy all over, like a dog-fight—unless it might be putting turpentine on a stray dog and setting fire to him, or tying a tin pan to his tail and see him run himself to death" (118–19).

The alternatives the law or the church might pose to this chaos are numerous, but instead of diminishing social injustice they tend to further it. The courts in *Great Expectations* reflect E.L. Woodward's observation that throughout most of the nineteenth century cheap and speedy justice was impossible in England.[19] Not only are the courts poorly run, as Pip discovers when asked by "an exceedingly dirty and partially drunk minister of justice" if he would like to "step in and hear a trial or so" (166), they are also unfairly run. Magwitch receives a longer prison sentence than Compeyson, his partner in crime, for reasons of open class prejudice. Rather than being considered the victim of society, Magwitch is punished for his unsavory background and poor appearance. As Compeyson's attorney tells the jury, " 'Here you has afore you, side by side, two persons as your eyes can separate wide; one, the younger, well brought up . . . one, the elder, ill brought up. . . . Can you doubt . . . which is much the worst one?' " (354). In *Huckleberry Finn* the legal system is even worse. Twain does not discuss such developments as the Fugitive Slave Act, which applied to the North and the South, or the Dred Scott decision, in which Justice Taney ruled that a Negro could not be considered a citizen of the United States. But it is clear from the way in which Jim is bought and sold, captured and held for a reward, that the law is only an obstacle to his freedom. The Duke and the Dauphin are correct in their belief that the surest way to get Jim down the Mississippi is to tie him "hand and foot with a rope, and lay him in the wigwam and say we captured him up the river, and were too poor to travel on a steamboat, so we got this little raft on credit from our friends and are going down to get the reward" (113).

Religion in *Great Expectations* and *Huckleberry Finn* is no less conspicuous by its absence as a positive force. In *Great Expectations* nothing is more apparent than the truth of Elie Halevy's observation in *The Age of Peel and Cobden* that most nineteenth-century Britains had little trouble combining the teachings of Christianity with the ethics of enlightened selfishness.[20] Pip is aware that those who talk most about the Church find his poverty reprehensible and his great expectations commendable, and it is logical that as a young man he should treat his economic rise as a form of conversion and his social ambition as a means to salvation. This worshipful attitude toward money pervades his childhood, especially on such occasions as his first visit to Miss Havisham:

I was soaped, and kneaded, and towelled, and thumped, and harrowed, and rasped until I really was quite beside myself.

When my ablutions were completed, I was put into clean linen of the stiffest character, like a young penitent into sackcloth, and was trussed up in my tightest and fearfullest suit. (52)

In *Huckleberry Finn* the church lends its support to a social order based on slavery and white supremacy (Miss Watson and the Widow Douglas have their slaves in for prayers). Consequently, in order for Huck to have genuine compassion for Jim, he must challenge the evangelical Calvinism to which he has been exposed. This is no easy task; Huck's decision to "go to hell" (180) for Jim's sake is a sign of his personal courage but also an indication of how trapped he is by false religious values that cause "something inside" him to say, " 'There was the Sunday school, you could a gone to it; and if you'd a done it they'd learnt you, there, that people that acts as I'd been acting about that nigger goes to everlasting fire' " (178). It never occurs to Huck to challenge the total basis of his religious upbringing even after he decides, "You can't pray a lie" (179). All he can do is put aside concern for his own future. "I shoved the whole thing out of my head; and said I would take up wickedness again, which was in my line, being brung up to it" (180).[21]

The process by which Pip and Huck finally achieve an understanding of the kind of world they live in does not reach fruition until the third sections of *Great Expectations* and *Huckleberry Finn*. Nonetheless, in the middle sections of both books there are at least two alternatives to social conformity that are always open to them. The first of these is reflected in the cynicism of Jaggers and Colonel Sherburn, and the second is reflected in the life that Wemmick and his father share on their island and Huck and Jim share on their raft.

Jaggers and Colonel Sherburn are ambiguous figures who, as a number of critics have shown, reflect divisions within their creators' minds. G. Robert Stange has observed, "As a surrogate of the artist, Jaggers displays qualities of mind—complete impassibility, all-seeing unfeelingness—which are the opposite of Dickens', but of a sort that Dickens may at times have desired."[22] Henry Nash Smith has made similar comments about Twain and Colonel Sherburn. "If one part of Mark Twain's mind could conceive of the happiness and freedom of two comrades on the raft, another part, just as true to his over-all view of life, speaks through Colonel Sherburn's denunciation of the Bricksville mob. . . ."[23] As a trial lawyer for the London underworld, Jaggers has a contempt for his clients that is equalled only by his contempt for those who sit in their judgment. The difficulty is that, although Jaggers's appraisal of human institutions and human nature is acute, his personal involvement in other men's affairs is virtually nonexistent. Jaggers is quite literally in the habit of "washing his hands" of the law (212), and his performance of this symbolic act demonstrates the degree to which his Olympian judgment of society depends on his detachment from it. The same is true of Colonel Sherburn, whose speech to the mob trying to lynch him is based on the premise, "The average man's a coward" (123). It is a premise not essentially different from Jagger's first words to Pip: " 'I have a pretty large experience of boys, and you're a bad set of fellows' " (83). Indeed, like Jaggers, Sherburn is trapped by his view of man. His shooting of Boggs reflects the cavalier ease with which he assumes the right to dispense justice, and his analysis of the South reveals the way in which he has used his moral awareness to avoid taking moral responsibility.

The need for separateness, which Jaggers and Colonel Sherburn feel, is not theirs alone, however. This same need explains much of the happiness that Pip shares with Wemmick and his father on their island and that Jim and Huck experience on their raft. The difference is that for Pip and Huck the lessons the island and the raft teach are exactly the opposite of those that Jaggers and Colonel Sherburn would have them learn. For the peace of mind both boys come to realize through Wemmick and Jim requires an openness rather than an immunity to human warmth.

IV   The final sections of *Great Expectations* and *Huckleberry Finn* are, as so many of Dickens's and Twain's critics have argued, the most crucial. In these sections Pip and Huck cease being primarily the victims and the observers of society and become actors in their own right. The moral choices they must make are still those they faced at the beginning of their adventures when their paths crossed those of an escaped convict and a runaway slave, but time has changed the roles they once fulfilled. Pip and Huck are no longer strangers to Magwitch and Jim, nor are they involved in their original father-son relationship with these men. It is they who have assumed the protective role normally associated with parenthood, and it is Magwitch and Jim, who, as outcasts, are now in a position of childlike defenselessness.

The reversal of these psychological roles is significant not only because it reflects the adult responsibilities Pip and Huck bear but because it reflects Dickens's and Twain's attitudes toward prison and slavery. For both authors the conditions of the criminal and the slave had come to symbolize the more general problems of social existence. As Lionel Trilling has observed, in the mind of Dickens "the idea of the prison was obsessive." He had personally experienced prison life through his father's three months in the Marshalsea, and he saw it as "the practical intrument for the negation of man's will which the will of society had contrived."[24] In *Great Expectations* Magwitch can recall his life only in terms of being "in jail and out of jail" (349). He has been born into prison life in the same way that Jim has been born into slavery and is a perfect example of Edmund Wilson's contention that "in his novels from beginning to end, Dickens is making the same point always: that to the English governing classes the people they govern are not real."[25] For Twain, slavery in the antebellum South was also not an exceptional condition, but in the words of Henry Nash Smith, "only an extreme example of the constraints imposed by that society on all its members, white as well as black."[26] In Huck's life, as in Pip's, the conditions of bondage and imprisonment are operative with only their formal attributes missing. Like Pip, Huck is alienated from his surroundings, trapped by the disapproval of those who raise him, and forced to act outside the law in order to defend his beliefs.

The decisions that Pip and Huck make when they finally side with Magwitch and Jim are, thus, more than gestures of sympathy toward two men who have no status in society. They imply recognition that similar forces affect their lives. How difficult it is for Pip and Huck to reach this awareness can be seen in the fact that, as far as Dickens and Twain were concerned, the naturalness of both boys was not by itself a guarantee of their virtue. Naturalness, as in the case of Orlick and Pap Finn, could be a negative quality, and even as a positive quality, it had limitations. Pip and Huck are extremely gentle children, but through most of *Great Expectations* and *Huckleberry Finn* they are influenced by the values of a corrupt society. Consequently, their renunciation of these values and their defense of Magwitch and Jim involves more than a return to the simple and intuitive responses of childhood. These responses have, in effect, proven inadequate, and they are replaced, not with more innocence, but with an extremely tough-minded humanism. In Pip's case this choice means accepting the loss of his great expectations. In Huck's case it means taking the risk of going to Hell.

There are also darker aspects to Pip's and Huck's inner life that are brought out by their loyalty to Magwitch and Jim. The most conspicuous of these is the guilt they bear. It is necessary to remember that Pip's adult reaction to Magwitch is initially one of "insurmountable aversion" (33) and that up to the time Jim is held prisoner on the Phelps's farm, Huck has moments when he thinks of him in terms of his value to Miss Watson: "I was stealing a poor old woman's nigger that hadn't ever done me no harm, and . . . I most dropped in my tracks I was so scared" (178). In this light Pip's and Huck's decision to help Magwitch and Jim may be seen as, above all else, atonement for their earlier lack of compassion. The nature of this atonement is made even clearer because there is a stop to the logical movement of events in *Great Expectations* and *Huckleberry Finn* that keeps both books from ending in total disaster.[27] Magwitch dies a natural death instead of being hanged, and Jim is set free in Miss Watson's will rather than returned to slavery. As a result, the consequences of Pip's and Huck's efforts to save Magwitch and Jim cease, in any literal way, to be a dramatic question. What remains important is the change within Pip and Huck: the difference between their confused and comic reactions to a criminal and a slave and their willingness to risk their own lives for Magwitch and Jim. In both stories this shift in emphasis from the actual to the symbolic is pervasive. Even Magwitch and Jim, who have the most to lose if Pip and Huck fail, realize the struggle to save them has at its deepest

level become one of the spirit. Magwitch is content to die as long
as Pip remains beside him, and Jim gives up his chance to escape
North for the sake of the wounded Tom Sawyer, who he believes is
as loyal to him as Huck.

V   The endings of *Great Expectations*
and *Huckleberry Finn* stress, however, not only the transformation
that takes place within Pip and Huck but important differences in
each story. The nature of these differences is apparent initially in the
style of the two books, both of which are narrated in the first person.
In Pip's case his speech, which in his boyhood is naively revealing
of his trustfulness, finally becomes that of a man who can get along
in society without adopting its cruelties. Huck's speech, on the other
hand, depends on a vernacular "prelapsarian in its innocence and
single-minded directness."[28] It presupposes not just a different set
of values from those of society but a new set of circumstances
(aesthetic and moral) for such values to become operative. These
differences are embodied in the role fulfilled by Wemmick's island-
home, Walworth, in *Great Expectations* and by the raft in *Huckleberry
Finn*. The island and the raft, as has already been shown, constitute
microcosmic communities in which mutual kindness is the basis of
all actions. But they also serve a second and more ordinary purpose,
which is determined by the needs they fulfill. In *Great Expectations* the
island gives Pip and Wemmick the strength to endure the everyday
world. Walworth is not an end in itself so much as a shelter allowing
Pip and Wemmick to move between two existences. Pip acknowledges this situation by returning to "Walworth again, and yet again"
(303) when he is in difficulty, and Wemmick makes this relationship
clear when he says, " 'No; the office is one thing, and private life is
another. When I go into the office, I leave the Castle behind me, and
when I come into the Castle, I leave the office behind me' " (210).
By contrast in *Huckleberry Finn* the protective function of the raft is
ultimately secondary. The raft becomes a world in itself, not a way
station that allows Jim and Huck to earn a living and then return to
safety. Unlike Pip and Wemmick, who have regular social respon-

sibilities, Huck and Jim rarely leave their raft unless they are forced to:

> We said there warn't no home like a raft, after all. Other places do seem so cramped up and smothery, but a raft don't. You feel mighty free and easy and comfortable on a raft. (99)

> It's lovely to live on a raft. We had the sky, up there, all speckled with stars, and we used to lay on our backs and look up at them. . . . (101)

By the end of *Great Expectations* and *Huckleberry Finn* these differences reach full dimension. After Magwitch's death and his own illness, Pip leaves England for a position in the Asian branch of a trading firm run by his friend Herbert Pocket. His desire is to escape the society he has known, but his retreat is limited and also bourgeois:

> I sold all I had, and put aside as much as I could, for a composition with my creditors. . . . Within a month, I had quitted England, and within two months I was clerk to Clarriker and Co., and within four months I assumed my first undivided responsibility.

> I must not leave it to be supposed that we were ever a great House, or that we made mints of money. We were not in a grand way of business, but we had a good name, and worked for our profits, and did very well. (488)

When Pip returns to England and has his chance meeting with Estella, he can still look forward to marrying her and settling down. His final accommodation is in marked contrast to Huck's unwillingness to return to St. Petersburg and the reward money Judge Thatcher is keeping for him: "I got to light out for the Territory ahead of the rest, because Aunt Sally she's going to adopt me and sivilize me and I can't stand it. I been there before"(245).

To insist on these differences is not, it must be stressed, to maintain that Pip reverts to his earlier callowness or that Huck is given a good chance for starting a new life in the West. Dickens makes it clear that the changes in Pip's character, his realization of the ways in which he has been "ungenerous and unjust" (487), are permanent, and Twain's pessimism is reflected both in his later story of "Huck Finn and Tom Sawyer Among the Indians"[29] as well as in Huck's observation that he can only get to the Territory "ahead" of the rest. The point of dwelling on these differences is that they show how Pip's escape turns out to be a strategic retreat, giving him the strength to return to society on better footing, and Huck's escape becomes in essence a declaration of independence, made at the risk of every material comfort he possesses.[30]

NOTES

1. Ellen Moers, "The 'Truth' of Mark Twain," *The New York Review of Books* 5 (January 20, 1966): 10.

2. See Walter Blair, *Mark Twain and Huck Finn* (Berkeley, 1960), pp. 61, 111, 310–14.

3. *The Autobiography of Mark Twain*, ed. Charles Neider (New York, 1959), pp. 174, 175.

4. For a different approach see Dennis S.R. Welland, "Mark Twain and the Victorians," *Chicago Review* 9 (Fall 1955): 101–109.

5. All page references are to the following paperback edition: Charles Dickens, *Great Expectations* (New York: Holt, Rinehart, Winston, 1948).

6. All page references are to the following paperback edition: Mark Twain, *Adventures of Huckleberry Finn* (Boston: Houghton Mifflin, 1958).

7. These distinctions are used with regard to Huckleberry Finn by Henry Nash Smith in *Mark Twain: The Development of a Writer* (Cambridge, Mass., 1962), pp. 121–2.

8. The dialectical quality of *Huckleberry Finn* is discussed by Henry Nash Smith in *Mark Twain: The Development of a Writer*, p. 113.

9. Erik Erikson, *Childhood and Society* (New York, 1950), pp. 237–44, 371–2.

10. See Mark Spilka, *Dickens and Kafka* (London, 1963), pp. 13–15.

11. Walter Houghton, *The Victorian Frame of Mind* (New Haven, 1963), pp. 341–5; William R. Taylor, *Cavalier and Yankee* (New York, 1960), pp. 140, 147.

12. James Cox, "Remarks on the Sad Initiation of Huckleberry Finn," *Sewanee Review* 62 (Summer 1954): 395.

13. Daniel G. Hoffman, *Form and Fable in American Fiction* (New York, 1961), pp. 333–4.

14. Dorothy Van Ghent, *The English Novel: Form and Function* (New York, 1965), p. 132.

15. T. S. Eliot, "Introduction," *Adventures of Huckleberry Finn* (London, 1950), pp. xii–xiii, xiii.

16. For further discussion of the Eden theme see J. Hillis Miller, *Charles Dickens: The World of his Novels* (Cambridge, Mass., 1958), p. 278; Kenneth Lynn, *Mark Twain and Southwestern Humor* (Boston, 1959), pp. 236–8.

17. Mark Twain, *The Adventures of Tom Sawyer* (New York, 1923), p. 54.

18. Ibid., p. 285.

19. E. L. Woodward, *The Age of Reform, 1815–1870* (Oxford, 1938), p. 453.

20. Elie Halevy, *The Age of Peel and Cobden: A History of the English People, 1841–1852* (London, 1947), pp. 454–5.

21. During the Civil War denominations in the North and South split over the question of slavery. (See Clifton Olmstead, *Religion in America: Past and Present* [Englewood Cliffs, 1961], p. 99.)

22. G. Robert Stange, "Expectations Well Lost: Dickens' Fable for his Time," *College English* 16 (October 1954): 16.

23. Henry Nash Smith, "Introduction," *Adventures of Huckleberry Finn* (Boston, 1958), p. xxvi.

24. Lionel Trilling, *The Opposing Self* (New York, 1955), pp. 52–3.

25. Edmund Wilson, "Dickens: The Two Scrooges," *Eight Essays* (Garden City, 1954), p. 30.

26. Henry Nash Smith, "Introduction," *Adventures of Huckleberry Finn*, p. xii.

27. For further analysis of the endings of the two books see Edgar Johnson, *Charles Dickens: His Tragedy and Triumph*, vol. 2 (New York, 1952), p. 993; Leo Marx, "Mr. Eliot, Mr. Trilling, and Huckleberry Finn," *American Scholar* 22 (Autumn 1953): 425–30.

28. Richard Bridgman, *The Colloquial Style in America* (New York, 1966), p. 10.

29. Mark Twain, "Huck Finn and Tom Sawyer Among the Indians," *Life* 65 (December 20, 1968): 33–48.

30. The Promethian quality of Huck's defiance is discussed by Ralph Ellison in *Shadow and Act* (New York, 1964), pp. 30–34.

7

Conclusion

In the last four chapters I have tried to make explicit what it means to define the uniqueness of American fiction in the terms put forward at the beginning of this essay. By attempting a detailed analysis of a limited number of well-known stories, I have hoped to show that what is needed is a reappraisal of the familiar, not a displacement of those texts generally assumed to constitute the great tradition in English and American fiction. In conclusion I should like to review, and hopefully to clarify, the three issues that seem to me of most importance in this comparison.

Form There is a long history in this country of wanting our national literature to reflect our independence, especially our political distance from England. As late as the nineteenth century, the problem of "being de-Britished" still had serious overtones for Americans. For Francis Parkman reliance on English standards weakened national character and meant, "The highest civilization of America is communicated from without instead of being developed from within and is therefore nerveless and unproductive." A publisher as prominent as Evert Duyckinck could not help inquiring, "From a people simple, brave, devout, what are we not to expect when these energies shall be turned in the direction of the National Literature?"[1] I think that in a more sophisticated and often uncomplimentary way the genre critics and those whom they have influenced also reflect an exaggerated concern for the Americanness of American literature. For in trying to describe the uniqueness of American fiction, genre criticism and its variants have found it necessary to postulate either a superform in which American fiction is depicted as a combination of qualities (which are not true for any one book and have no viable organizing principle) or a fragmented form in which single qualities are said to reveal the essence of American fiction (despite the fact that other qualities are often of equal or greater importance).

Without abandoning the many specific insights into American fiction that genre criticism and its variants have provided, it is, I believe, possible to see what is unique about the form of American fiction in much different terms: terms not based on the idea that we are *necessarily* in a position to account for the uniqueness of American fiction if we locate qualities characteristic of it or indigenous to it or both important in their own right and present in a number of American stories. Stated in a nutshell, my argument is that distinguishing American from English fiction requires analysis of the total process by which certain qualities common to both traditions are given a different emphasis: specifically, the way nineteenth-century American fiction gives an ultimate importance (and textual dominance) to certain ideational or visionary concerns that finally makes these concerns superior to or situationally transcendent of the social context in which they appear and the way nineteenth-century English fiction gives a qualified importance (and textual limitation) to such concerns that finally makes them coextensive with or subordinate to the social context in which they appear.

In critical practice what this requires, I believe, is analyzing the form of American and English fiction in a fuller and more active way than genre criticism and its variants allow: in this case, replacing a concern with categories, like romance or myth or symbolism, with a concern for the manner in which American and English fiction *actually* move in different directions. It is for this reason that I have focused so much attention on Scott and Cooper and the implications of their historical vision, Hawthorne and Eliot and their treatment of the fall, Melville and Hardy and their preoccupation with the problem of nil, Dickens and Twain and their interest in childhood and society. For I think these comparisons show how the approach to form used here takes into account the scope of American and English fiction and the points where they are closest, and by so doing, provides a way of coming to grips with the artistic process—one might almost say rhythm—in American fiction that gives it organic unity and enables us to distinguish it.

Concern   Although on occasion a critic like Richard Chase will speak of the hybrid quality of American and English fiction, and thus seem about to deal with the problem of balance in the two traditions,[2] the thrust of genre criticism and its variants is in the opposite direction. The view of American fiction they advance is one in which abstractions and symbolic constructs dominate to the point where concern with society is regarded as a tangential matter for the American writer. I have sought to counter this view in a number of ways but most fully with the assertion that the differences between American and English fiction can be likened to the differences between a spire and a dome, both of which have a solid foundation, but each of which has a different sweep—that of the spire sending it above and then beyond its source; that of the dome sending it above and back to its source.

At this point I would like to carry the analogy further, lest it be thought that in arguing that visionary concerns are more important than societal concerns in American fiction I have simply refurbished the criticism I originally take to task. The primary divergence between my views and those I oppose lies, I think, in the fact that my distinction emphasizes not the distance or tangential nature of the visionary and societal concerns in American and English fiction but their closeness: how they are related, how their separation, when it does occur, is a tenuous and subtle process. I do not find that in the nineteenth century American fiction deals in single-minded fashion with abstractions, nor do I find that English fiction in this same period is narrowly preoccupied with social reality. Moreover, I think that the relationship between these two forces accounts for what is most unsettling and most complex in the two traditions: their preoccupation with contradictions and their ability to transcribe them into the terms of art without necessarily resolving them.[3] In *Rob Roy* and *The Prairie* the official heroes opt for social comfort, but the most memorable quality of their lives stems from their involvement with men who reject modern society. In *The Scarlet Letter* and *Adam Bede* religious understanding is a paramount concern, but it cannot resolve or undo personal tragedy. In *Pierre* and *Jude the Obscure* two young men acquire the courage to face a series of metaphysical and social dilemmas, but in the end their courage cannot give them the will to live. In *Great Expectations* and *Huckleberry Finn* escape from society is seen as perfectly justified (in the case of Twain's story, even poetic), yet it holds no promise of lasting happiness.

What it means finally to see the visionary and societal concerns of American and English fiction in terms of their relationship to each other is, I think, best put into perspective by Henry James's observation in his preface to *The American:*

> By what art or mystery, what craft of selection, omission or commision, does a given picture of life appear to us to surround its theme, its figures and images, with the air of romance, while another picture close behind it may affect us as steeping the whole matter in the element of reality? . . . I doubt if any novelist, for instance, ever proposed to commit himself to one kind or the other with as little mitigation as we are sometimes able to find for him. The interest is greatest—the interest of his genius, I mean, and of his general wealth—when he commits himself in both directions; not quite at the same time or to the same effect, but by some need of performing his whole possible revolution, by the law of some rich passion in him for extremes.[4]

The rich passion for extremes that James would have us take into account is the very quality in American and English fiction that gives substance to its romantic and imaginative flights as well as its social analysis. But what it demands in turn is a critical approach that does not minimize this passion, even when the advantages of doing so are that the critic is put in a position to make distinctions that appear more striking.

History   In order to account for the romanticism and abstractness they find in American fiction, the genre critics and most of those whom they have influenced have turned to American history for an explanation. Their basic argument is that in a young country like America society has shown itself to be thin and writers have not had before them enough material for producing the social novel. This argument seems to me inaccurate on historical as well as on literary grounds.

To begin with, although it is a truism that American society has not developed many of the formal structures and class distinctions of European society, it is absolutely untrue that American society has been sufficiently bland or, as the work of C. Wright Mills shows, sufficiently free from the influence of power elites to provide no basis for the social novel.[5] Basil March's observation in *A Hazard of New Fortunes* that "there's no use pretending that we haven't a nobility; we might as well pretend we haven't first class cars in the presence of a vestibuled Pullman" provides apt illustration of the opportunities for dealing with class and manners in America and the way critics have denied such opportunities existed. One need only look at seventeenth-century New England or the South before the Civil War to see other equally conspicuous chances the American writer had for developing the social novel.

More to the point, the social-thinness interpretation of American fiction and American history obscures the use the American writer did make of his environment and his past. Here I have in mind not simply the European qualities in books like *The Blithedale Romance* and *The Gilded Age* but the broad sense of American history revealed in American fiction. Indeed, when we take into account only the four texts with which this study deals, the result is still a remarkably inclusive and insightful view of American history. It is a view that begins with Hawthorne's treatment of Puritan culture and its effect on all areas of life—from religion, to dress, to sexual relations —continues with Cooper's analysis (similar to that of Frederick

Jackson Turner) of the frontier as a source of political and social values, moves on to Twain's description of the South prior to the Civil War, and concludes with Melville's protrait of the destruction of an aristocratic Dutch family when the heir to its fortune cannot abide by tradition or adopt to the ways of a highly impersonal New York City.

Finally, if we accept the relationship between American history and American fiction found in genre criticism and so many of its variants, it becomes impossible to deal with a whole set of additional artistic problems. We cannot explain why American writers living in Europe and presented with a complex society continued writing the kind of fiction they did in their own country. We can do little to escape the notion that certain types of historical conditions almost inevitably produce only one type of fiction. We must accept the proposition that the American writer was constantly forced by poverty of circumstances to create a different brand of fiction than he wanted. The result, as I have previously argued, is an inaccurate view of American fiction. But in the long run it is also more than that. For such theorizing dehumanizes American fiction, making us lose sight of the fact that its fullness depends, as Hawthorne wrote of one of his stories, on "airy and unsubstantial threads, intermixed with others, twisted out of the commonest stuff of human existence . . . not widely different from the texture of all our lives."[6]

NOTES

1. Quotations from Richard Bridgman, *The Colloquial Style in America* (New York, 1966), pp. 43, 44.

2. Chase ends up defining the American novel (which in his view is a romance) primarily in terms of a "more or less formal abstractness . . . a willingness to abandon moral questions or to ignore the spectacle of man in society" and then adding the proviso, "the romances of our literature, unique only in their peculiar but widely differing amalgamation of novelistic and romantic elements." The result is that Chase is left with a static analysis: one that seems to acknowledge the hybrid quality of American fiction

but in actuality treats the romantic elements of it in isolation—as if they alone defined the tradition. (*The American Novel and its Tradition* [New York, 1957], pp. ix, 14.)

3. For a discussion of the question of reductive literary criticism see Frederick Crews, "Anaesthetic Criticism," *New York Review of Books* 14 (February 26, 1970): 31–5 and (March 12, 1970): 49–52.

4. Henry James, *The Art of the Novel* (New York, 1962), pp. 30–31.

5. See in particular C. Wright Mills, *The Power Elite* (New York, 1959), pp. 11–20. There Wright discusses how the fact that America did not pass through a feudal epoch and never had a high church or court nobilities contributed to the rise and prestige of its upper strata and power elite.

6. Nathaniel Hawthorne, *The Marble Faun* (Columbus, 1968), p.6.

$\mathcal{T}$he Gateway of Language

I It is unfortunate that Richard Bridgman's review of Richard Poirier's *A World Elsewhere: The Place of Style in American Literature* should be characterized by the following passage: "The study of prose style is a demanding one, and no more so than when one tries to understand the role style plays in the protean world of American letters. But the churning disorder of Richard Poirier's *A World Elsewhere* . . . offers the student no assistance."[1] The effect of such criticism is to obscure the complementary nature of Poirier's *A World Elsewhere* and Bridgman's *The Colloquial Style in America,* to make us miss the way both studies give not only new emphasis to the role of language in American literature but significantly widen our understanding of how American fiction works.

Like Leo Marx in his seminal essay, "The Vernacular Tradition in American Literature," Bridgman sees the colloquial tradition as pervasive.[2] But he goes far beyond Marx in his treatment of it, finding it crucial not only to Mark Twain and the local colorists but to Cooper, Hawthorne, Melville, James, and Hemingway.[3] The key to Bridgman's analysis of the colloquial tradition is his assertion that "in spite of genuine reservations about the possibility of discussing a national prose style, I believe that one can still affirm the following propositions with some confidence":

1) American prose style changed significantly between 1825 and 1925.
2) On the whole the change was toward greater concreteness of diction and simplicity in syntax.
3) The change was initiated primarily in dialect pieces and in fictional dialogue.
4) Toward the end of the century writers became increasingly conscious of the techniques of colloquial writing.
5) These techniques were then stylized to accentuate the following characteristics of colloquial style:
   a) stress on the individual verbal unit,
   b) a resulting fragmentation of syntax, and
   c) the use of repetition to bind and unify.[4]

Bridgman does go on to qualify this statement, "The characteristics that ultimately identify the colloquial style—stress, fragmentation, and repetition—are not in themselves unique to it. But in aggregate and in heavy concentrations, they do signal a major and identifiable style."[5] But his qualification is not a means of compromising his thesis or denying it historical specificity, "Literary change is never linear, but in general it can be said that this movement began when dialogue was the servant of the narrative, and that it continued until narrative prose was dominated by the habits of dialogue: or, it began with Hawthorne, ended with Hemingway."[6] Bridgman is able to locate the colloquial style in the "drayhorse dialogue" of Hester Prynne and Arthur Dimmesdale, in the "hash of dialect, Biblical simplicity, romantic effusion, old saws, and didacticism" of Natty Bumppo, in the "archaic, Old Testament idiom" of Ahab, as well as in the "single-minded directness" of Huck's speech.[7] His explication, while often brief, as in the case of Hawthorne, Cooper, and Melville, is never unconvincing, and he is particularly successful in demonstrating the parallels between the colloquial style in the major novels of American fiction and the colloquial style in such lesser works as George Washington Harris's *Sut Lovingood.*[8]

The point at which Bridgman's analysis becomes questionable is when we try to discover how the colloquial tradition as he defines it is unique to America. To start with the comic colloquial tradition: certainly, there are typically American jokes, and as Constance Rourke long ago pointed out, there is a relationship between American humor and American national character.[9] Yet with regard to language patterns it is virtually impossible to locate a comic, colloquial style that is distinctly American. For comedy based on linguistic peculiarities in region and class or extensive use of the vernacular, we can always turn to the fiction of Dickens. Moreover, it is not necessary to use minor characters or minor scenes in Dickens to illustrate this point. In a novel like *Great Expectations* this kind of comedy is embodied in such telling episodes as Joe Gargery's verbal (and moral) assault on Jaggers. Indeed, Joe's climactic outburst is dramatically effective because his speech, in contrast to Jaggers's legalistic and precise syntax, is a combination of grammatical errors, anger, slang, incoherence, and repetition (all of which are carefully interwoven by Dickens): " 'Which I meantersay,' cried Joe, 'that if you come into my place bull-baiting and badgering me, come out! Which I meantersay as sech, if you're a man, come on! Which I meantersay that what I say, I meantersay and stand or fall by!' "[10]

On a non-comic level the same kinds of comparative problems arise with regard to Bridgman's thesis. For although it is clear that in American fiction the colloquial style is often uniquely American in subject (the frontier) or in regional speech patterns (those of a Tennessee mountaineer), it does not follow that an exclusively American colloquial style is revealed by the abandonment of standard English or in the use of language drawn from dialogue and dialect and based on stress, fragmentation, and repetition. Such linguistic forms are also important in nineteenth-century English fiction.

George Eliot's *Adam Bede* provides a classic example of a novel in which the kinds of speech patterns Bridgman is discussing are used to achieve a simplicity and directness of expression. Dinah Morris, the heroine of *Adam Bede,* is preoccupied with plainness of speech and dress, and the sermon she delivers at the start of Eliot's novel is moving not because of its theological depths but because of a naturalness in which the "simple things she said seemed like novelties, as a melody strikes us with new feeling when we hear it sung by the pure voice of a boyish chorister":[11]

"Why, you and me, dear friends are poor. We have been brought up in poor cottages, and have been raised on oat cake, and lived coarse. . . . We are just the sort of people that want to hear good news. . . . We know very well we are altogether in the hands of God: we didn't bring ourselves into the world, we can't keep ourselves alive while we're sleep-

ing; the daylight, and the wind, and the corn, and the cows to give us milk
—everything we have comes from God.''[12]

In Adam Bede's case the homely quality of his speech is even
more evident, and the very factors (concreteness, stress, repetition, dialect spelling) that Bridgman finds characteristic of the
colloquial style in America are used to convey the practical nature of his religious beliefs:

> "And there's such a thing as being over-speritial; we must have be-
> side Gospel i' this world. Look at the canals, an' th' aqueducs, an' th'
> coal-pit engines, and Arkwright's mills there at Cromford; a man
> must learn summat beside Gospel to make them things, I reckon.
> . . . And this is my way o' looking at it: there's the sperrit o' God in
> all things and all times—weekday as well as Sunday . . . and i' the
> figuring and the mechanics.''[13]

Among nineteenth-century English writers, Dickens and Eliot
were not, however, alone or unique in their use of the colloquial
style. Thomas Hardy was acutely aware of its possibilities and relied
on it for his characterization of rustics like Gabriel Oak and Diggory
Venn.[14] Scott, too, used the colloquial, both in minor ways and, as
the following passage from *Rob Roy* indicates, to reflect psychological and social conditions:

> it appears to me that in his case, and in that of some other Highlanders
> whom I have known, that, when familiar and facetious, they used the
> Lowland Scottish dialect,—when serious and impassioned, their
> thoughts arranged themselves in the idiom of their native language; and
> in the latter case, as they uttered the corresponding ideas in English, the
> expressions sounded wild, elevated, and poetical.[15]

It is Bridgman's failure to give serious consideration to such uses
of the colloquial that limits the value of his study, and in comparative terms causes it to be misleading; but it makes no sense—indeed,
it is destructive of what he has done—to pursue a criticism of his
work beyond this point. For more far-reaching answers to the question of style in American fiction, we can instead turn to Richard
Poirier's *A World Elsewhere: The Place of Style in American Literature.*

II

Even more than Bridgman, Poirier is disturbed by analyses that "name without explaining."[16] It is impossible to separate his attack on past criticism of American literature from his assertion, "The classic American writers try through style temporarily to free the hero (and the reader) from systems, to free them from the pressures of time, biology, economics, and from the social forces which are ultimately the undoing of American heroes. . . ."[17] At the center of Poirier's argument is his contention that the usual environmental or historical explanations for the uniqueness of American fiction are inadequate:

> One of the first English novels comparable to the American fiction of civilization and the frontier is *Robinson Crusoe,* but it is indicative of the American emphases of Cooper, of Mark Twain, of Thoreau . . . that Defoe's novel is a sort of idyllic parable of man's gaining merely economic control over an environment out of which he could try to make anything he chose. A true born Englishman, he has no interest whatever in the merely visionary possession of landscape. . . . This comparison suggests what is, for other reasons, too, an inescapable conclusion: the strangeness of American fiction has less to do with the environment in which a novelist finds himself than with the environment he tries to create for his hero. . . . [18]

Poirier is, however, no less dissatisfied with analyses of American fiction that are based on genre:

> The categorization of American fiction into novels, and more numerously, into romances, even when the categories are made subtle by Richard Chase in *The American Novel and Its Tradition* has tended to obscure the more challenging questions. . . . When scenes occur in American literature that by standards of ordinary life are foolish, preposterous, or sexually irregular they are usually interpreted in one of three all relatively unsatisfactory ways: they are translated into psycho-sexual terms with the implication that because we have discovered something covert we have therefore revealed "more" than the obvious, idealistic, or ideological reading. Or they are discussed merely as metaphoric expressions of one or another myth in romantic or American literature, with little, usually no attention to the fact that the expression of this myth often does unwittingly raise questions about sex and psychology. Or they are much more simply disposed of with the observation that after all they belong to a romance, since of course they could not have occurred in a novel.[19]

For Poirier, the principal defect of all the readings he criticizes is the "tendency to treat experiences in fiction as if somehow they existed independently of the style which creates them and which creates, too, the environment in which these experiences make or do not make sense."[20] Only after one gets beyond "the superficiality of genre criticism and the limitations of other more sophisticated categorizations,"[21] is it possible to see what, in Poirier's view, is unique about American literature and above all American fiction: "the effort to stabilize certain feelings and attitudes that have, as it were, no place in the world, no place at all except where a writer's style can give them one":[22]

> What is centrally important is the evidence almost everywhere in American literature of an idealistic effort to free the heroes' and the readers' consciousness from categories not only of conventional moralities but also of mythopoeic interpretation.
>
> The result is a struggle to create through language an environment in which the inner consciousness of the hero-poet can freely express itself, an environment in which he can sound publicly what he privately is.[23]

Unlike Bridgman, Poirier is not concerned with revealing a particular linguistic pattern in American prose so much as demonstrating a particular effect achieved by the prose:

> I have tried to locate the phenomenon in style, in the rhythms and sounds of sentences . . . with the only materials—language—with which he [the writer] can try to "build" a world. As it is used in this book, the word style refers to grammar, syntax, and tropes only by way of defining some more significant aspect of style: the sounds, identities, and presences shaped by these technical aspects of expression.[24]

The crucial differences between *The Colloquial Style* and *A World Elsewhere* arise, however, because Poirier's views can bear comparative scrutiny with regard to nineteenth-century American and English fiction. Indeed, the only modification one has to make of this point is that in English fiction there is also a concern, although a lesser one, with building worlds elsewhere, and hence the stylistic differences between the two traditions are often not as clear as Poirier indicates.[25]

How tightly this generalization holds can be seen by testing it with four passages (two American and two English) that do not appear in *A World Elsewhere* but are representative of nineteenth-century American and English fiction. The first of these passages is from *The Scarlet Letter* and is a description of Dimmesdale's election-day sermon:

> The eloquent voice, on which the souls of the listening audience had been borne aloft, as on the swelling waves of the sea, at length came to a pause. There was a momentary silence, profound as what should follow the utterance of oracles. Then ensued a murmur and half-hushed tumult; as if the auditors, released from the high spell that had transported them into the region of another's mind, were returning into themselves, with all their awe and wonder still heavy on them. . . . Now that there was an end, they needed other breath, more fit to support the gross and earthly life into which they relapsed, than the atmosphere which the preacher had converted into words of flame, and had burdened with the rich fragrance of his thought.[26]

The second passage is from *Adam Bede* and is a description of Dinah Morris's sermon on the village green:

> But now she had entered into a new current of feeling. Her manner became less calm, her utterance more rapid and agitated, as she tried to bring home to the people their guilt, their willful darkness, their state of disobedience to God—as she dwelt on the hatefulness of sin, the Divine holiness, and the sufferings of the Savior. . . . who was waiting and watching for their return.
>
> There was many a responsive sigh and groan from her fellow Methodists, but the village mind does not easily take fire, and a little smouldering vague anxiety, that might easily die out again, was the utmost effect Dinah's preaching had wrought in them at present.[27]

The external similarities of these passages are striking. They begin with water images, conclude with fire images, and describe the differences between the speaker and his audience as well as the religious quality of the sermons delivered. Yet the closer we look at the passages, the more apparent it becomes that Poirier's "world elsewhere" distinction applies. Although both sermons deal with states of awareness that cannot be comprehended in economic or political terms, it is clear that Dinah's sermon is in part defined (and limited) by her traditional references to sin and love. The content of Dimmesdale's sermon is, on the other hand, never disclosed, nor can it be. For Dimmesdale is not merely reminding his congregation of sin and love (the subject of his sermon is "the relation between the Deity and the communities of mankind"). Like an "oracle," he is "transporting" them beyond verbal references to a "region" of the imagination. The use of imagery in the two passages bears out this difference. In Eliot's novel the "current" refers to the flow of Dinah's "feeling." But in Hawthorne's novel the "sea" is part of an extended metaphoric description of how the Puritans are "borne aloft" by an overwhelming spiritual force. Thus, Dimmesdale's sermon suggests not only the outward qualities of a Pentecostal vision, it "converts" the atmosphere into "words of flame." By contrast, the "fire" in Dinah's sermon arouses "a smouldering vague anxiety," which reveals that her listeners, unlike Dimmesdale's, are barely moved at this point.[28]

Similar comparisons can be made on the basis of passages in *Huckleberry Finn* and *Great Expectations*. The first passage is an extended description of Huck and Jim on the raft:

> so Jim he got out some corn dodgers and buttermilk, and pork and cabbage, and greens—there ain't nothing in the world so good when its cooked right—and whilst I eat my supper we talked, and had a good time.
>
> It's lovely to live on a raft. We had the sky, up there, all speckled with stars, and we used to lay on our backs and look up at them and discuss about whether they was made, or only just happened. . . . [29]

The second passage consists of two different descriptions of Pip at Wemmick's island-home:

> We had a loin of pork for dinner, and greens grown on the estate, and I nodded at the Aged with a good intention whenever I failed to do it drowsily.
>
>   Nor was there any drawback in my little turret bedroom, beyond there being such a very thin ceiling between me and the flagstaff, that when I lay down on my back in bed, it seemed as if I had to balance that pole on my forehead all night.[30]

Like the previous passages cited, these, too, are strikingly similar. The account of eating, the mood of relaxation, the positioning of both speakers on their backs (hence their natural description of what is above them) show the degree to which the raft and Waldover provide a haven from ordinary society. Yet Poirier's world elsewhere distinction applies in this case as well. In *Huckleberry Finn*, in contrast to *Great Expectations*, there is a rhythmic listing (not just a naming) of food that is ritualistic in its insistence on what constitutes a good meal, and it corresponds to the fact that Huck's supper (prepared by Jim) is lingered over and represents a communion between them (Pip's supper basically increases his comfort and drowsiness). Similarly, while Pip goes to sleep describing the snugness around him (which in many ways parallels the kind of strategic retreat he is seeking), Huck looks up and evokes a pastoral vision of the night that in its wonder and metaphor of a "sky speckled with stars" suggests, as Leo Marx has noted, a "sense of solidarity with the physical universe" that "acquires the intensity of a religious experience."[31]

The difficulty with Poirier's book is that he does not subject his own views to this kind of comparative scrutiny. To raise this objection is not, of course, to suggest that Poirier, whose method is illustrative, should have used these particular comparisons, but it is to point out that the only extended comparison in *A World Elsewhere* is between Mark Twain and Jane Austen, and it is a comparison that analyzes writers who are so palpably different that we are left without a clue as to how Poirier's analysis would work with writers as similar in style and theme as Dickens and Twain. This defect in Poirier's study can, however, be gotten around. What cannot be gotten around is that the achievement Poirier wishes to analyze by examining style cannot be limited to style. Although the works he is concerned with achieve their uniqueness through the medium of language, it does not follow that it is because of language alone that they are unique. The Hawthorne and Twain passages previously analyzed demonstrate the degree to which factors other than style contribute to the making of a world elsewhere. In *The Scarlet Letter* Dimmesdale's vision and new power of speech are the consummation of a struggle that has been going on through the story. They are dependent upon a series of psychological and spiritual revelations that he had experienced, and their dramatic effect is inseparable from Hawthorne's careful and climactic arrangement of Dimmesdale's appearances before the Puritans. The same textual complexity is true of *Huckleberry Finn*. Huck's pastoral vision cannot be separated from the emphasis given his psychological relationship to Jim (which exists despite the historical condition of Jim's slave status) or from the series of contrasts Twain makes between life on the raft and life in the towns along the Mississippi.

It is, of course, to Poirier's credit that the points he raises about style go beyond style, but under these circumstances the only way in which the true value of *A World Elsewhere* can be properly realized is by rejecting its conclusions as final or sufficient, by seeing that they provide a gateway rather than a framework for understanding the uniqueness of American fiction.

NOTES

1. Richard Bridgman, "Richard Poirier: *A World Elsewhere: The Place of Style in American Literature,*" *Nineteenth-Century Fiction* 22 (June 1967): 97.

2. Leo Marx, "The Vernacular Tradition in American Literature," *Studies in American Culture,* ed. Joseph J. Kwiat and Mary C. Turpie (Minneapolis, 1960), pp. 109-22.

3. Many of the qualities Bridgman treats in terms of the colloquial style in America, Perry Miller treats in terms of the "plain style," which he traces to the Puritans. See *Nature's Nation* (Cambridge, Mass., 1967), pp. 208-40.

4. Richard Bridgman, *The Colloquial Style in America* (New York, 1966), p. 12.

5. Ibid., p. 21.

6. Ibid., p. 62.

7. Ibid., pp. 65, 66, 69, 10.

8. For a negative treatment of the colloquial style in American fiction see Marius Bewley, *The Complex Fate* (New York, 1967), pp. 2-3.

9. Constance Rourke, *American Humor* (New York, 1955), pp. 9-10.

10. Charles Dickens, *Great Expectations* (New York, 1948), p. 143.

11. George Eliot, *Adam Bede* (Boston, 1968), p. 24.

12. Ibid., pp. 22-3.

13. Ibid., p. 9.

14. For further treatment of this aspect of Hardy's style see Albert Guerard, *Thomas Hardy* (Norfolk, 1964), pp. 122-7.

15. Sir Walter Scott, *Rob Roy* (Boston, 1956), p. 359.

16. The quotation itself is by Richard Ohmann and is used by Richard Bridgman at the start of *The Colloquial Style in America,* p. 3.

17. Richard Poirier, *A World Elsewhere: The Place of Style in American Literature* (New York: Oxford University Press, 1966), p. 5.

18. Ibid., pp. 8-9.

19. Ibid., pp. 10–11.

20. Ibid., p. 11.

21. Ibid. p. 12.

22. Ibid., p. ix.

23. Ibid., p. 35.

24. Ibid., p. viii.

25. There are points in his study where Poirier touches on this question of emphasis, but they are not as thorough as one would wish. (See pp. 16-17, 38.)

26. Nathaniel Hawthorne, *The Scarlet Letter* (Boston, 1960), p. 246.

27. George Eliot, *Adam Bede*, p. 25.

28. Later on Dinah's sermon does have a more powerful effect on her "hearers," but even at this point Eliot's language does not have the intensity of Hawthorne's. (See p. 26.)

29. Mark Twain, *Adventures of Huckleberry Finn* (Boston, 1958), pp. 99, 101.

30. Charles Dickens, *Great Expectations*, pp. 377, 211.

31. Leo Marx, *The Machine in the Garden* (New York, 1964), p. 335.

Appendix B

$\mathcal{R}$*evising the Trilling Thesis*

Like Marius Bewley's *The Eccentric Design*, A. N. Kaul's *The American Vision* begins with an analysis of the following passage from Lionel Trilling's essay, "Manners, Morals, and the Novel":

> Now the novel as I have described it has never really established itself in America. Not that we have not had very great novels but that the novel in America diverges from its classic intention, which, as I have said, is the investigation of the problem of reality beginning in the social field. The fact is that American writers of genius have not turned their minds to society. . . . the reality they sought was only tangential to society.[1]

But although Kaul finds that Trilling's "perceptive formulation" has a suggestiveness that goes beyond the requirements of the context in which it appears,"[2] he does not pursue the thin-soil argument that the form of American fiction evolved as it did because "for the American artist there was no social surface responsive to his touch."[3] He is unequivocal in asserting that the explanation for the uniqueness of American fiction is to be found "not in the social reality of America but rather in the novelists' conception of it":[4]

> If American writers were unable to create the social novel, so the argument goes, the explanation lies in the fact that, apart from their own failings, America could boast no social scenes subtle or picturesque enough to tempt the artist's palette.
> This view is neither accurate nor wholly satisfactory. As I have already indicated, the American novelists were quite capable of writing in the

best manner of European fiction. They have left considerable proof of this ability, as well as of the availability of necessary materials in such portions of their work as the Albany scenes of *The Blithedale Romance* (not to mention the Salem of *The Seven Gables*), and the urban descriptions of *Pierre*.[5]

Kaul's "more positive account of the American novelists' concern with society and values,"[6] thus, marks a revision rather than an extension of Lionel Trilling's theories on the nature and origins of American fiction. Whether or not his revision escapes equally serious faults of its own is another question, however: one that demands close scrutiny.

Like Trilling, Kaul sees the question of society as fundamental to any attempt to distinguish American fiction. But he is not willing to equate manners and institutions with social reality:

> If the American writers of genius did not turn their minds to social description, is it not necessary to examine their attitude to the whole question of "society"? In order to understand their genius do we not need to look more closely at what constituted the social reality of nineteenth-century America? . . . did it [their pursuit of reality] lead them to imaginative constructs of a life and values which can be called "social" in the best sense of the term?[7]

In Kaul's view it is the "problems of social technique and organization" rather than "tension between the classes" which are at the center of society in American fiction, and consequently he regards the social dissatisfactions of the American novelist as very different from those of a writer preoccupied with romantic escape.[8] "Cooper, Hawthorne, Melville, and even the Mark Twain of *Huckleberry Finn* . . . . did not employ their imaginations in the construction of fairy tales or fantasies," Kaul argues.[9] All four writers were instead "deeply concerned with both the society of their times and an ideal conception of social relationships," and "the consequent interplay between actual and ideal social values" constitutes an important source of "their continuing vitality."[10] Kaul still acknowledges that in "the works of all these four novelists there comes undoubtedly a stage at which they diverge from what Trilling has called the 'classic intention' of the novel. . . . 'the investigation of the problem of reality beginning in the social field.' "[11] But this acknowledgment, depending as it does on Kaul's assertion that the American novelists' concern with "the existing social order" and "an ideal society" are "inseparably connected with each other,"[12] is not at all the same as Trilling's contention that the American novelist sought a reality "only tangential to society."

Kaul sees concern with an ideal society manifesting itself in nineteenth-century American fiction in a variety of ways, e.g., "the relationship between Natty and Chingachgook," "the values that govern the relationship between Ishmael and Queequeg," "the community Huck and Jim create on the raft";[13] and he finds this concern consistent with "the oldest and most persistent of American beliefs": ones that have their religious origin in John Winthrop's sermon, "A Model of Christian Charity," and their secular extension in the founding of Brook Farm.[14] Kaul does not, however, limit his analysis to American fiction: "A good way to define the distinctive character of the nineteenth-century American novel is to approach it through fiction which was produced contemporaneously in England. The comparison is particularly relevant, since the two countries were bound by ties of a common language and cultural heritage."[15] For Kaul the importance of such a comparison is that it reveals how "preoccupations with social questions" led American novelists, in contrast to English novelists, to "ideas of total overhauling and intimations of ideal community life." "Their imagination worked in terms of radical substitutes rather than localized improvements. Concerned with the basic fact of human relationship, which alone can provide a foundation of social organization, they were visionaries rather than reformers."[16] This point is one that Kaul expands into the following generalization:

> Society then does not exist in the mid-nineteenth century American novel either as a ubiquitous presence or as the all-important determinant of human life and attitudes. This is the fact which finally distinguishes American from European fiction. The reformist intention of the English novelists, the fact that they regarded their work as an appeal addressed to society itself, is only a humane corollary which follows from the attitude of regarding the existing social order as the most potent factor in the human situation.[17]

What Kaul has demonstrated through his pursuit of this line of argument is considerable. He has succeeded in removing the basic genre implications of the Trilling thesis, and in turn persuasively argued that, "if the American novelists of the nineteenth century did not follow the techniques of their English contemporaries, it is not because they were less concerned with the perfection of human society but because they were more so."[18] Moreover, he has managed to call attention to the social depth of the American novel and still avoid the deterministic argument that American fiction is a direct reflection of American history. Finally, he has opened up new and important literary territory by his insistence that "criticism has tended to deny the social theme of the classic American novel any serious consideration beyond the point where it breaks away from the realism of the European novel."[19]

The difficulty is that the virtues of Kaul's study cannot be separated from defects that become increasingly serious the further one analyzes his understanding of the relative uniqueness of American fiction. This area is ironically one in which Kaul's theoretical understanding seems especially subtle:

> If we say that it is open to the novelist to explore experience in three different spheres: the subjective world of the individual and of his private relations, the domain of relationships dictated by social institutions, and finally the larger and less easily realizable realm of man's relationship to the constitution and working of certain cosmic forces essentially beyond human control, and if we call them the personal, the social, and the metaphysical dimensions of experience, we will be able to state the difference between English and American fiction in a simple form. It can scarcely be maintained that the fictional themes of any particular culture or time monopolize any one of these aspects to the exclusion of the other two. . . . Nevertheless, one can assert safely that whereas European fiction of the mid-nineteenth century works out its themes predominantly in social terms, the contemporary American imagination concerns itself directly with the world of man's personal and metaphysical relations.[20]

Kaul's practical understanding of textual balance or what it means to work "predominantly" in one "sphere" turns out to be misleading and rigid, however, when applied to European fiction: "The distinctive characteristic of American fiction is not that it wholly disregards existing social reality but that it is not wholly preoccupied with it. Unlike European fiction it is not confined within the limits of the given social field."[21] The implications of this passage (that the European novelist was "wholly preoccupied" and confined" by the social field) are not unintended, and the following quotation makes Kaul's position even clearer: "The dramas of Bal-

zac, Dostoevsky, and Emily Brontë, as much as those of Dickens, are
wholly worked out in terms of the social institutions and values of
the nineteenth century."[22] There is no serious recognition on
Kaul's part that these novelists are often torn by the demands of
more than one "sphere" or that their work frequently consists of
what Donald Fanger has called "a principled deformation of reality."[23] It is not necessary, however, to put Kaul's argument to the
harsh test of trying to explain the Grand Inquisitor scene "wholly"
in terms of "the social institutions and values of the nineteenth
century." One can instead focus on the most relevant comparison
for American fiction, that of English fiction, and on the writer whom
Kaul finds most representative of English fiction at mid-nineteenth
century, the Charles Dickens of the 1840s and 1850s.

The results in Dickens's case are no less decisive, for far from
being "wholly preoccupied" with society, Dickens is in conflict with
those who can see no further than their immediate surroundings. At
the start of *Bleak House* he notes the similarity between the world of
manners and the world of institutions ("the world of fashion and the
Court of Chancery are things of precedent and usage; oversleeping
Rip Van Winkles") with the express purpose of emphasizing their
limits: "It is not a large world. . . . But the evil of it is, that it is a
world wrapped up in too much jeweller's cotton and fine wool, and
cannot hear the rushing of the larger worlds, and cannot see them
as they circle round the sun."[24] For Dickens, not seeing beyond the
social world was, as this passage illustrates, a form of deafness and
blindness. It is inaccurate to say, as Kaul does on the basis of his
analysis of *Dombey and Son,* that Dickens "focuses his criticism entirely on social institutions—business, church, and family."[25] There
are far greater possibilities that concern Dickens, as the attention he
gives to the sea in *Dombey and Son* reveals, "And the voices in the
waves are always whispering to Florence in their ceaseless murmer-
ing of love—of love, eternal and illimitable, not bounded by the
confines of this world, or by the end of time, but ranging still beyond
the sea, beyond the sky, to the invisible country far away!"[26] Dickens's attitude toward society is simply not comparable to that of
novelists who, "insofar as they attacked it [society], their tendency
was toward arousing sympathy for the practical reform of the institutions they exposed."[27] Throughout his fiction Dickens continually
shows the need for reform and the difficulty of relying on it. He
understood that the state was not about to change its ways suffi-

ciently to benefit its Oliver Twists, and he saw a basic inhumanness
in a figure like Thomas Gradgrind, who thought only in terms of
reform or systematic social change.[28]

When one moves beyond the Dickens of these years to the Dickens of the 1860s or to George Eliot or to Thomas Hardy, the
narrowness of Kaul's argument becomes even more apparent. For
although books like *Great Expectations* and *Middlemarch* and *Jude the
Obscure* are intensely concerned with social questions and the need
for reform (in the prison system, medicine, and the University), they
are not circumscribed by any of these matters. Even *Middlemarch*, in
which Eliot's heroine, Dorothea Brooke, marries "an ardent public
man working well in those times when reforms were begun with a
young hopefulness of immediate good," centers on the more complex problems of "young and noble impulse struggling amidst the
conditions of an imperfect social state."[29]

With American fiction, on the other hand, Kaul's faults lie in the
opposite direction. He is so anxious to show how the American
writer was concerned with "the theme of society rather than with
any particular social theme" that he underestimates the role that
institutions play in the American novel.[30] One can see the form his
error takes by looking again at *Bleak House*, which is dominated by
two institutions: that of the family as a unit of wealth, power, and
tradition (symbolized by a house like Sir Leicester Dedlock's Ches-
ney Wold) and that of the English judicial system (symbolized by the
case of Jarndyce v. Jarndyce). There is no adequate accounting for
similar forces within American fiction by Kaul, who argues that to
the "creative imagination" in America "freedom and supremacy of
the individual constituted not a battle to be fought and won but
rather a generally accepted principle."[31] Yet the supremacy of the
individual is battled over in American fiction. If there are no Ded-
locks, there are numerous families whose wealth, power, and traditions (also symbolized by a house) serve to limit rather than increase
personal freedoms. This influence is reflected in Judge Temple's
towering "mansion," which gave "a fashion to the architecture of
the country," the Pyncheon house, "with seven acutely peaked gables facing towards various points of the compass," the Glendinning
house at Saddle Meadows, "the embowered and high-gabled old
home of his [Pierre's] fathers," and the Grangerford's "old-fash-
ioned double log house" with "so much style."[32] The law in nineteenth-century American fiction is a similarly powerful institution.

In *The Pioneers,* which closes after Natty's trial for hunting a deer out of season, or *The Scarlet Letter,* which begins with Hester's release from jail, or *Huckleberry Finn,* in which Jim has no legal claim to freedom, the law is not just a metaphor for human cruelty but the means by which society enforces judgments that violate the most deeply-felt personal freedoms.

It is not, however, until Kaul begins to discuss *Moby Dick* that the lengths to which he is prepared to carry his views on the "comparative absence of institutionalized relations" in American fiction become apparent.[33] In his preliminary discussion of *Moby Dick,* Kaul maintains that it takes place in an "institutional vacuum," and then he goes on to assert as primary evidence for this opinion the "void which separates (almost literally) Melville's detailed description of the whaling industry from the vaster reaches of his theme."[34] Yet, this void is not what Kaul suggests. To begin with, Ahab recognizes that he faces the possibility of mutiny if his voyage is unsuccessful, and he is continually forced to take into account or play on the feelings of his crew, "Ahab plainly saw that he must still in good degree continue true to the natural, nominal purpose of the *Pequod's* voyage, observe all customary usages; and not only that, but force himself to evince all his well-known passionate interest in the general pursuit of his profession."[35] More importantly, the whaling industry and the social structure of the *Pequod* form a significant contrast with the feelings governing Ishmael's and Queequeg's relationship. It is clear that the values of the whaling industry are exactly the opposite of those that Queequeg and Ishmael affirm. Melville is not at all hesitant about equating the whaling industry with the system of racial and industrial exploitation occurring in America in the 1850s. After describing how the three mates of the *Pequod* have harpooners of a different race and country, he observes:

> at the present day not one in two of the many thousand men before the mast employed in the American whale fishery, are American born, though pretty nearly all the officers are. Herein it is the same with the American whale fishery as with the American army and military and merchant navies, and the engineering forces employed in the construction of the American Canals and Railroads. The same, I say, because in these cases the native American literally provides the brains, the rest of the world as generously supplying the muscles.[36]

Melville then extends his references to American history even further when in the same chapter on "Knights and Squires," he describes the crew of the *Pequod* (which numbers thirty, the same
number of states in the Union at this time) as *"Isolatoes . . .* not
acknowledging the common continent of men, but. . . . federated
along one keel."[37]

To read *Moby Dick* and ignore the way in which these references
suggest the uniqueness and the importance of the ties that bind
Queequeg and Ishmael is to overlook much of what Melville has
done. Yet Kaul would read not only Melville in this manner but
Cooper and Twain, for example. He sees the unhappy endings to
the novels of all three writers reflecting an "attitude of 'betrayed
expectancy,' " a consequence of the "nineteenth-century mistake of
assuming an easy relation between ideals and reality."[38] But novels
like *The Prairie* and *Huckleberry Finn,* no less than *Moby Dick,* do not
lead to the conclusion that the American writer "expected to see his
ideas materialize immediately and on the spot."[39] In *The Prairie*
Natty Bumppo constantly stresses his age and the fact that he has
moved west in order to escape the unavoidable rush of settlers. It
comes as no surprise that he asserts, "I am without kith or kin.
. . . when I am gone there will be an end of my race."[40] In a different
way the same sense of fatality hangs over *Huckleberry Finn.* Once the
raft floats by Cairo, there can be no realistically happy ending for
Jim and Huck, nor is the likelihood of their permanently escaping
the cruelty they encounter along the river suggested. Twain has
prepared the way for Huck's admission that he can only hope to get
to the Territory "ahead" of the rest.[41]

In view of these and similar circumstances the final result of
Kaul's analysis is that it turns out to be a mixed critical blessing. His
corrections of the Trilling thesis are of enormous importance, but
at the same time they are inseparable from a reading of nineteenth-
century American and English fiction that narrows, even under-
mines, the societal vision within both traditions.

NOTES

1. A. N. Kaul, *The American Vision: Actual and Ideal Society in Nineteenth-Century Fiction* (New Haven: Yale University Press, 1964), p. 2.
2. Ibid.
3. Marius Bewley, *The Eccentric Design* (New York, 1963), p. 15.
4. A. N. Kaul, *The American Vision*, p. 52.
5. Ibid., p. 313.
6. Ibid., p. 3.
7. Ibid., p. 4.
8. Ibid., pp. 5, 66.
9. Ibid., p. 6.
10. Ibid., pp. 4, 4-5.
11. Ibid., p. 307.
12. Ibid., P. 310.
13. Ibid., pp. 137, 272, 292.
14. Ibid., pp. 318, 9, 36.
15. Ibid., p. 47.
16. Ibid., p. 53.
17. Ibid., p. 57.
18. Ibid., p. 312.
19. Ibid., p. 310.
20. Ibid., pp. 59-60
21. Ibid., pp. 307-8.
22. Ibid., p. 57.
23. Donald Fanger, *Dostoevsky and Romantic Realism* (Cambridge, Mass., 1965), p. 15.
24. Charles Dickens, *Bleak House* (London, 1951), p. 8.
25. A. N. Kaul, *The American Vision*, p. 58.
26. Charles Dickens, *Dombey and Son* (London, 1950), p. 811.
27. A. N. Kaul, *The American Vision*, p. 48.
28. Dickens was no less outspoken in his public statements on reform. In a speech delivered at the Birmingham and Midland Institute, he quoted with approval the following passage from Buckle's *History of Civilization:* "They may talk as they will about reforms which Government has introduced and improvements to be expected from legislation, but whoever will take a wider and more commanding view of human affairs will soon discover that such hopes are chimerical." (Quoted in Humphrey House, *The Dickens World* [London, 1961], p. 173.)
29. George Eliot, *Middlemarch* (Boston, 1956), pp. 610, 612.
30. A. N. Kaul, *The American Vision*, p. 67.
31. Ibid., p. 71.

32. James Fenimore Cooper, *The Pioneers* (New York, 1967), pp. 30, 31; Nathaniel Hawthorne, *The House of the Seven Gables* (Boston, 1964), p. 9; Herman Melville, *Pierre* (New York, 1957), p. 1; Mark Twain, *Adventures of Huckleberry Finn* (Boston, 1958), pp. 81, 85.

33. A. N. Kaul, *The American Vision*, p. 64.

34. Ibid., pp. 58, 64.

35. Herman Melville, *Moby Dick* (New York, 1964), p. 210.

36. Ibid., pp. 117-18.

37. Ibid., p. 118.

38. A. N. Kaul, *The American Vision*, pp. 319, 320.

39. Ibid., p. 319.

40. James Fenimore Cooper, *The Prairie* (New York, 1950), p. 450.

41. Mark Twain, *Adventures of Huckleberry Finn*, p. 245.

Bibliography

The items in this bibliography are secondary sources. They do not include the novels around which this study is based. These novels are cited in the footnotes of the chapters in which they appear and are paperback texts, available to the general reader.

General Critical Studies

Adams, Robert. *Nil: Episodes in the Literary Conquests of Void During the Nineteenth Century.* New York, 1966.

Anderson, Quentin. *The Imperial Self.* New York, 1971.

Auerbach, Erich. *Mimesis.* Garden City, 1957.

Baritz, Loren. *City on a Hill.* New York, 1964.

Bewley, Marius. *The Complex Fate.* New York, 1967.

_____ *The Eccentric Design.* New York, 1963.

Bradbury, Malcolm. "Towards a Poetics of Fiction." *Novel* 1 (Fall 1967): 45–52.

Bridgman, Richard. *The Colloquial Style in America.* New York, 1966.

Briggs, Asa. *The Making of Modern England.* New York, 1965.

Brooks, Van Wyck. *New England: Indian Summer.* New York, 1940.

Cecil, David. *Victorian Novelists.* Chicago, 1958.

Chase, Richard. *The American Novel and its Tradition.* Garden City, 1957.

Edel, Leon. *The Modern Psychological Novel.* New York, 1964.

Fanger, Donald. *Dostoevsky and Romantic Realism.* Cambridge, Mass., 1965.

Feidelson, Charles, Jr. *Symbolism and American Literature.* Chicago, 1962.

Fiedler, Leslie. *Love and Death in the American Novel.* New York, 1960.

Frye, Northrop. *Anatomy of Criticism.* Princeton, 1957.

Fussell, Edwin. *Frontier: American Literature and the American West.* Princeton, 1965.

Green, Martin, *Re-Appraisals: Some Commonsense Readings in American Literature.* New York, 1967.

Hardy, Barbara. *The Appropriate Form.* London, 1964.

Hirsch, David. "Reality, Manners, and Mr. Trilling." *Sewanee Review* 72 (July-September 1964): 420-32.

Hoffman, Daniel G. *Form and Fable in American Fiction.* New York, 1961.

Holland, Norman. *The Dynamics of Literary Response.* New York, 1968.

Holloway, John. *The Victorian Sage.* New York, 1965.

Houghton, Walter E. *The Victorian Frame of Mind.* New Haven, 1957.

Howard, Leon. *Literature and the American Tradition.* Garden City, 1960.

Howe, Irving. *Politics and the Novel.* Cleveland and New York, 1962.

Jones, Howard Mumford. *O Strange New World.* New York, 1964.

Kaul, A. N. *The American Vision: Actual and Ideal in Nineteenth-Century Fiction.* New Haven, 1964.

Kazin, Alfred. *On Native Grounds.* Garden City, 1956.

Kettle, Arnold. *An Introduction to the English Novel.* 2 vols. New York and Evanston, 1960.

Krieger, Murray. *The Tragic Vision.* Chicago, 1966.

Lawrence, D. H. *Studies in Classic American Literature.* Garden City, 1951.

Leavis, F. R. *The Great Tradition.* New York, 1963.

Levin, Harry. *The Power of Blackness.* New York. 1960.

Lewis, R. W. B. *The American Adam.* Chicago, 1955.

McLoughlin, William G. "Pietism and the American Character." *American Quarterly* 17 (Summer 1965): 163-86.

Marcus, Steven. *The Other Victorians.* New York, 1967.

Marx, Leo. *The Machine in the Garden.* New York, 1964.

Matthiessen, F. O. *American Renaissance.* New York, 1957.

Maxwell, D. E. S. *American Fiction: The Intellectual Background.* New York, 1965.

Miller, Perry. *Errand into the Wilderness.* New York, 1964.

Miller, Perry. *Nature's Nation.* Cambridge, Mass., 1967.

Parrington, Vernon L. *Main Currents in American Thought.* 2 vols. New York, 1954.

Poirier, Richard. *A World Elsewhere: The Place of Style in American Literature.* New York, 1966.

Porte, Joel. *The Romance in America: Studies in Cooper, Poe, Hawthorne, Melville, and James.* Middletown, 1969.

Praz, Mario. *The Hero in Eclipse in Victorian Fiction.* London, 1956.

Pritchett, V. S. *The Living Novel and Later Appreciations.* New York, 1967.

Rahv, Philip. *The Myth and the Powerhouse.* New York, 1966.

Rourke, Constance. *American Humor.* Garden City, 1955.
Sanford, Charles L. *The Quest for Paradise: Europe and the American Moral Imagination.* Urbana, 1961.
Schwartz, Delmore. "The Duchess' Red Shoes." *Partisan Review* 20 (January-February 1953): 55-73.
Smith, Henry Nash. *Virgin Land.* New York, 1950.
Stevenson, Lionel. *The English Novel: A Panorama.* Boston, 1960.
Sussman, Herbert L. *Victorians and the Machine: The Literary Response to Technology.* Cambridge, Mass., 1968.
Tanner, Tony. *The Reign of Wonder.* New York, 1965.
Tillotson, Kathleen. *Novels of the Eighteen-Forties.* Oxford, 1961.
Trilling, Lionel. *The Liberal Imagination.* Garden City, 1950.
Van Ghent, Dorothy. *The English Novel: Form and Function.* New York, 1953.
Watt, Ian. *The Rise of the Novel.* Berkeley and Los Angeles, 1962.
Wellek, René. *Concepts of Criticism.* London, 1964.
Williams, Raymond. *Culture and Society : 1780-1950.* Garden City, 1960.
Winters, Yvor. *In Defense of Reason.* Denver, 1960.

Sir Walter Scott

Cockshut, A.O.J. *The Achievement of Walter Scott.* London, 1969.
Daiches, David. "Scott's Achievement as a Novelist," *Literary Essays.* London, 1956, pp. 88-121.
Davie, Donald. *The Heyday of Sir Walter Scott.* New York, 1961.
Grierson, Herbert. *Sir Walter Scott, Bart.* London, 1938.
Hart, Francis R. *Scott's Novels: The Plotting of Historical Survival.* Charlottesville, 1966.
Hillhouse, James T. *The Waverly Novels and their Critics.* Minneapolis, 1937.
Johnson, Edgar. *Sir Walter Scott.* 2 vols. New York, 1970.
Lockhart, J. G. *Memoirs of the Life of Sir Walter Scott.* 5 vols. Boston, 1901.
Lukacs, George. *The Historical Novel.* London, 1962.
Muir, Edwin. *Scott and Scotland.* London, 1936.
Welsh, Alexander. *The Hero of the Waverly Novels.* New Haven, 1963.

James Fenimore Cooper

Beard, James Franklin, ed. *The Letters and Journals of James Fenimore Cooper.* 6 vols. Cambridge, Mass., 1960-1968.
Dekkar, George. *James Fenimore Cooper the Novelist.* London, 1967.
Grossman, James. *James Fenimore Cooper.* New York, 1949.
House, Kay. *Cooper's Americans.* Columbus, 1966.
Jones, Howard Mumford. "Prose and Pictures: James Fenimore Cooper," *Tulane Studies in English,* vol. 3 (1952), pp. 133-54.

Levin, David. *History as a Romantic Art.* New York, 1959.

Lounsbury, Thomas. *James Fenimore Cooper.* Boston, 1882.

Parkman, Francis. "The Works of Fenimore Cooper," *Francis Parkman: Representative Selections,* ed. Wilbur Schramm. New York, 1938, pp. 202-17.

Philbrick, Thomas. *James Fenimore Cooper and the Development of American Sea Fiction.* Cambridge, Mass., 1961.

Ringe, Donald A. *James Fenimore Cooper.* New York, 1962.

Ross, John F. *The Social Criticism of Fenimore Cooper.* Berkeley, 1933.

Shulenberger, Arvid. *Cooper's Theory of Fiction.* Lawrence, 1955.

Spiller, Robert. *Fenimore Cooper: Critic of his Times.* New York, 1931.

Twain, Mark. "Fenimore Cooper's Literary Offenses," *The Shock of Recognition,* ed. Edmund Wilson. New York, 1955, pp. 582-94i.

Nathaniel Hawthorne

Arvin, Newton. *Hawthorne.* Boston, 1929.

Carpenter, Frederic J. "Scarlet A Minus." *College English* 5 (January 1944): 173-80.

Cowley, Malcolm. "Five Acts of *The Scarlet Letter.*" *College English* 19 (October 1957): 11-16.

Crews, Frederic. *The Sins of the Fathers: Hawthorne's Psychological Themes.* New York, 1966.

Davidson, Edward H. *Hawthorne's Last Phase.* New Haven, 1948.

Fick, Leonard J. *The Light Beyond: A Study of Hawthorne's Theology.* Westminster, 1955.

Fogle, Richard. *Hawthorne's Fiction: The Light and the Dark.* Norman, 1952.

Gerber, John C. "Form and Content in *The Scarlet Letter.*" *New England Quarterly* 17 (March 1944): 25-52.

James, Henry. *Hawthorne.* Ithaca, 1956.

Kazin, Alfred. "The Ghost Sense." *New York Review of Books* 11 (October 24, 1968): 26-8.

Leavis, Q. D. "Hawthorne as Poet." *Sewanee Review* 59 (Spring and Summer Issues 1951): 179-205, 426–58.

Male, Roy. *Hawthorne's Tragic Vision.* Austin, 1957.

Pearce, Roy Harvey, ed. *Hawthorne Centenary Essays.* Columbus, 1964.

Ryskamp, Charles. "The New England Sources of *The Scarlet Letter.*" *American Literature* 31 (November 1959): 257-73.

Stewart, Randall. *Hawthorne.* New Haven, 1948.

Turner, Arlin. *Nathaniel Hawthorne.* New York, 1961.

Waggoner, Hyatt H. *Hawthorne.* Cambridge, 1963.

Warren, Austin. *Rage for Order.* Ann Arbor, 1959, pp. 84-103.

George Eliot

Bennett, Joan. *George Eliot, Her Mind and her Art.* Cambridge, England, 1948.

Bissell, Claude T. "Social Analysis in the Novels of George Eliot." *English Literary History* 18 (September 1951): 221-39.

Creeger, George R. "An Interpretation of *Adam Bede.*" *English Literary History* 23 (September 1956): 218-38.

Gregor, Ian, and Brian Nicholas. *The Moral and the Story.* London, 1962.

Haight, Gordon S., ed. *The George Eliot Letters.* 7 vols. New Haven, 1954.

Hardy, Barbara. *The Novels of George Eliot.* London, 1959.

Harvey, W. J. *The Art of George Eliot.* New York, 1962.

Leavis, F. R. *"Adam Bede,"* Anna Karenina and Other Essays. New York, 1969, pp. 49-58.

Paris, Bernard J. *Experiments in Life: George Eliot's Quest for Values.* Detroit, 1965.

Stephen, Leslie. *George Eliot.* New York, 1902.

Stump, Reva. *Movement and Vision in George Eliot's Novels.* Seattle, 1959.

Thale, Jerome. *The Novels of George Eliot.* New York, 1959.

Willey, Basil. *Nineteenth Century Studies.* New York, 1949.

Herman Melville

Arvin, Newton. *Herman Melville.* New York, 1957.

Bowen, Merlin. *The Long Encounter: Self and Experience in the Writings of Herman Melville.* Chicago, 1960.

Braswell, William. *Melville's Religious Thought.* New York, 1959.

Chase, Richard. *Herman Melville: A Critical Study.* New York, 1949.

Franklin, H. Bruce. *The Wake of the Gods: Melville's Mythology.* Stanford, 1966.

Howard, Leon. *Herman Melville.* Los Angeles and Berkeley, 1951.

Leyda, Jay. *The Melville Log.* 2 vols. New York, 1951.

Metcalf, Eleanor Melville. *Herman Melville: Cycle and Epicycle.* Cambridge, Mass., 1953.

Miller, Perry. *The Raven and the Whale.* New York, 1956.

Moorman, Charles. "Melville's *Pierre* and the Fortunate Fall." *American Literature* 25 (March 1953): 13-30.

Mumford, Lewis. *Herman Melville: A Study of his Life and Vision.* New York, 1962.

Nelson, Raymond J. "The Art of Herman Melville: The Author of Pierre." *Yale Review* 59 (December 1969): 197-214.

Olson, Charles. *Call Me Ishmael.* New York, 1947.

Stern, Milton. *The Fine Hammered Steel of Herman Melville.* Urbana, 1957.

Thompson, Lawrance. *Melville's Quarrel with God.* Princeton, 1952.

Wright, Nathalia. *"Pierre:* Herman Melville's Inferno." *American Literature* 32 (May 1960): 167-81.

Thomas Hardy

Beach, Joseph Warren. *The Technique of Thomas Hardy.* New York, 1962.
Brown, Douglas. *Thomas Hardy.* London, 1961.
Cecil, David. *Hardy the Novelist.* New York, 1946.
Firor, Ruth A. *Folkways in Thomas Hardy.* Philadelphia, 1931.
Guerard, Albert. *Thomas Hardy.* New York, 1964.
Hardy, Florence Emily. *The Early Life of Thomas Hardy, 1840-1891.* New York, 1928.
————*The Later Years of Thomas Hardy, 1892-1928.* New York, 1930.
Hawkins, Desmond. *Thomas Hardy.* London, 1950.
Holland, Norman, Jr. *"Jude the Obscure:* Hardy's Symbolic Indictment of Christianity." *Nineteenth Century Fiction* 9 (June 1964): 50–60.
Howe, Irving. *Thomas Hardy.* New York, 1967.
Lawrence, D. H. "Study of Thomas Hardy," *Phoenix.* London, 1961, pp. 398–516.
Mizener, Arthur. *"Jude the Obscure* as Tragedy." *Southern Review* 6 (Summer 1940): 193–213.
Weber, Carl J. *Hardy of Wessex.* New York, 1940.
Webster, Harvey Curtis. *On a Darkling Plain.* Chicago, 1947.
Wing, George. *Thomas Hardy.* London, 1963.

Charles Dickens

Cockshut, A. O. J. *The Imagination of Charles Dickens.* London, 1961.
Collins, Philip. *Dickens and Crime.* Bloomington, 1968.
Engel, Monroe. *The Maturity of Dickens.* Cambridge, Mass., 1959.
Fielding, K. J. *Charles Dickens: A Critical Study.* Boston, 1964.
Ford, George H. *Dickens and his Readers.* Princeton, 1955.
Forster, John. *The Life of Charles Dickens.* 2 vols. London, 1927.
Hagan, John H., Jr. "Structural Patterns in Dickens's *Great Expectations."* *English Literary History* 21 (March 1954): 54–66.
House, Humphrey. *The Dickens World.* London, 1960.
Hynes, Joseph A. "Image and Symbol in *Great Expectations." English Literary History* 30 (September 1963): 258–92.
Johnson, Edgar. *Charles Dickens: His Tragedy and Triumph.* 2 vols. New York, 1952.
Marcus, Stephen. *Dickens: From Pickwick to Dombey.* New York, 1965.
Miller, J. Hillis. *Charles Dickens: The World of His Novels.* Cambridge, Mass., 1958.

Moyhahan, Julian. "The Hero's Guilt: The Case of *Great Expectations.*" *Essays in Criticism* 10 (January 1960): 60–79.

Orwell, George. "Charles Dickens," *A Collection of Essays.* Garden City, 1954, pp. 55–110.

Smith, Grahame. *Dickens, Money, and Society.* Berkeley and Los Angeles, 1968.

Spilka, Mark. *Dickens and Kafka.* Bloomington, 1963.

Stange, G. Robert. "Expectations Well Lost: Dickens' Fable for his Time." *College English* 16 (October 1954): 9–17.

Wilson, Edmund. "Dickens: The Two Scrooges," *Eight Essays.* Garden City, 1954, pp. 11–91.

Mark Twain

Blair, Walter. *Mark Twain and Huck Finn.* Berkeley and Los Angeles, 1960.

Branch, Edgar. *The Literary Apprenticeship of Mark Twain.* Urbana, 1950.

Brooks, Van Wyck. *The Ordeal of Mark Twain.* New York, 1920.

Cox, James. "Remarks on the Sad Initiation of Huckleberry Finn." *Sewanee Review* 62 (Summer 1954): 389–405.

De Voto, Bernard. *Mark Twain's America.* Chatauqua, 1933.

Foner, Philip. *Mark Twain: Social Critic.* New York, 1958.

Howells, William Dean. *My Mark Twain.* New York, 1917.

Lynn, Kenneth. *Mark Twain and Southwestern Humor.* Boston, 1959.

Marx, Leo. "Mr. Eliot, Mr. Trilling, and Huckleberry Finn." *American Scholar* 22 (Autumn 1953): 423–40.

Smith, Henry Nash. *Mark Twain: The Development of a Writer.* Cambridge, Mass., 1962.

Taylor, William R. *Cavalier and Yankee.* New York, 1961.

Index